Thro... ...e
SHADOwLANDS

Through the
SHADOWLANDS

The Love Story of
C. S. LEWIS *and* JOY DAVIDMAN

Brian Sibley

Revell
Grand Rapids, Michigan

© 1985, 1994 by Brian Sibley and the British Broadcasting Corporation

Published by Fleming H. Revell
a division of Baker Publishing Group
P.O. Box 6287, Grand Rapids, MI 49516-6287

New trade paperback edition published 2005

Originally published in the United Kingdom by Hodder and Stoughton under the title
Shadowlands.

Second printing, June 2005

Printed in the United States of America

Library of Congress Cataloging-in-Publication Data
Sibley, Brian.
    [Shadowlands]
    Through the shadowlands : the love story of C. S. Lewis and Joy Davidman /
Brian Sibley.
        p.   cm.
    "Previously published in the United Kingdom by Hodder and Stoughton
under the title Shadowlands"—T.p. verso.
    Includes bibliographical references.
    ISBN 0-8007-3070-4 (pbk.)
    1. Lewis, C. S. (Clive Staples), 1898–1963—Marriage. 2. Authors, English—
20th century—Biography. 3. Authors, American—20th century—Biography.
4. Authors' spouses—Great Britain—Biography. 5. Christian converts from
Judaism—Biography. 6. Anglicans—England—Biography. 7. Davidman, Joy—
Death and burial. 8. Christian biography—England. 9. Davidman, Joy—
Marriage. I. Title.
PR6023.E926Z89 2005
823'.912—dc22
[B]   2005042758

For
Roger Lancelyn Green and June
because they were friends of
Jack and Joy
and are now friends of mine

Contents

Acknowledgments

The author and publisher are grateful to the following copyright holders for permission to reproduce copyright material:

The Bodley Head Ltd., for extracts from *Out of the Silent Planet*, *Perelandra*, *The Magician's Nephew*, and *The Last Battle* by C. S. Lewis.

Brandt and Brandt, on behalf of the Estate of William Lindsay Gresham, for extracts from "From Communist to Christian" and from the letters of William Gresham.

Curtis Brown Ltd., on behalf of the Estate of Helen Joy Lewis, for extracts from *Letter to a Comrade*, *Anya*, *Weeping Bay*, "The Longest Way Round," "Girl Communist," and from the letters of Joy Davidman; on behalf of the Estate of W. H. Lewis for extracts from W. H. Lewis's biography of C. S. Lewis; on behalf of C. S. Lewis Pte Ltd., for extracts from the preface to *Essays Presented to Charles Williams*, introduction to *Smoke on the Mountain*, letters, journals, and juvenile story "To Mars and Back"; also on behalf of John Wain for an extract from "C. S. Lewis" in *Encounter*.

William Collins Sons and Co. Ltd., for extracts from *The Problem of Pain*, *Broadcast Talks*, *The Screwtape Letters*, *Miracles*,

Mere Christianity, The Lion, the Witch and the Wardrobe, The Voyage of the "Dawn Treader," The Silver Chair, Narrative Poems, and *C. S. Lewis at the Breakfast Table* (ed. J. T. Como).

William B. Eerdmans Publishing Co., for extracts from *Letters to an American Lady.*

Roger Lancelyn Green, for extracts from "C. S. Lewis" in *Puffin Annual No. 1*; and Roger Lancelyn Green and Walter Hooper, for extracts from *C. S. Lewis: A Biography.*

Houghton Mifflin Company, for extracts from *J. R. R. Tolkien: A Biography* and *The Inklings* by Humphrey Carpenter and 'On Fairy Stories' in *Tree and Leaf* by J. R. R. Tolkien.

Macmillan Publishing Co., for extracts from *And God Came In* by Lyle W. Dorsett.

Marion E. Wade Collection, Wheaton College, Wheaton, Illinois, for extracts from *Brothers and Friends: The Diaries of Major Warren Hamilton Lewis* (ed. Clyde S. Kilby and Marjorie Lamp Mead).

Oxford University Press, for extracts from *The Allegory of Love* by C. S. Lewis.

Westminster Press, for extracts from *Smoke on the Mountain* by Joy Davidman.

Winston Press, for extracts from *A Grief Observed* by C. S. Lewis.

Introduction

A man is ill-advised," C. S. Lewis once said, "to write a book on any living author. There is bound to be at least one person and there are probably several who inevitably know more about the subject than ordinary research will discover. Far better to write about the unanswering dead. . . ."

In the case of a book about C. S. Lewis, however, the fact that he is no longer alive does not actually make the task any easier, since there are still many people who will know more about the subject than any outsider, however well-intentioned.

Besides, so much (in all probability, *too* much) has already been written about the man and his work. Indeed, C. S. Lewis currently looks set to join that select—but unfortunate—band of men whose entire works are outnumbered by works about them.

What justification, then, can there be for adding yet another book to the pile? Only this: to tell more completely than it has been told before the story of a remarkable relationship between two astonishing people—Jack Lewis and Joy Davidman—and, since that relationship lasted only a very few years, to tell something of their separate lives during the years before they met.

Anyone wishing to piece together as much of this story as possible would need to refer to at least a dozen different published works, including biographies, journals, and correspondence. My aim has been to draw together the relevant passages from these sources into one chronological account.

Believing, as I do, that the best form of biography is autobiography, I have endeavored, wherever possible, to let the principal players in this drama (who were all far better writers than I) recount their own stories.

I am, therefore, much indebted to the respective copyright holders, which are listed separately; and especially to Elizabeth Stevens of Curtis Brown. I also wish to acknowledge the invaluable assistance given me by two indispensable published sources: Roger Lancelyn Green and Walter Hooper's book, *C. S. Lewis: A Biography*, and Lyle W. Dorsett's biography of Joy Davidman, *And God Came In*; I extend my grateful thanks to their authors and recommend their books to all who would know more about Jack and Joy.

In writing this book I have also drawn on a number of interviews and conversations I had—while researching the television film *Shadowlands*—with the following people: Father Peter Bide, June and Roger Lancelyn Green (on various occasions and during several telephone conversations), Douglas Gresham, Father Walter Hooper (in person and in many helpful letters), Pauline Baynes, and Kaye Webb. Their help, so generously given, is much appreciated.

Assistance of various kinds (ranging from the provision of scarce books to stimulating conversations and correspondence) was provided by Humphrey Carpenter, Lyle W. Dorsett, Dr. Selwyn H. Goodacre, Marjorie Lamp Mead, Richard Parlour, Father Douglas Reed, Raphael Shaberman, Norman Stone, David Thompson, and Chad Walsh. And this is as good a place as any to say *thank you* to Patricia Hammond White who—when I was eight (and had measles)—lent me *The Lion, the Witch and the Wardrobe*, so beginning my interest in the books of C. S. Lewis; and to my mother who, several years later, fostered that interest with copies of *Mere Christianity* and *The Screwtape Letters*.

Finally, I must thank Magnus Magnusson and family, without whose kindness and hospitality this book might never have been written; and Alex Platt, without whose painstaking work it would most certainly never have gotten typed!

Brian Sibley, June 1985

. . . Then Aslan stopped, and the children looked into the stream. And there, on the golden gravel of the bed of the stream, lay King Caspian, dead, with the water flowing over him like liquid glass. . . . And all three stood and wept. Even the Lion wept: great Lion-tears, each tear more precious than the earth would be if it was a single solid diamond. . . .

"Son of Adam," said Aslan, "go into that thicket and pluck the thorn that you will find there, and bring it to me."

Eustace obeyed. The thorn was a foot long and sharp as a rapier.

"Drive it into my paw, son of Adam," said Aslan, holding up his right fore-paw and spreading out the great pad towards Eustace.

"Must I?" said Eustace.

"Yes," said Aslan.

Then Eustace set his teeth and drove the thorn into the Lion's pad. And there came out a great drop of blood, redder than all redness that you have ever seen or imagined. And it splashed into the stream over the dead body of the King. And the dead King began to be changed. His white beard turned to grey, and from grey to yellow, and got shorter and vanished altogether; and his sunken cheeks grew round and fresh, and the wrinkles were smoothed, and his eyes opened, and his eyes and lips both laughed, and suddenly he leaped up and stood before them—a very young man, or a boy. . . . And he rushed to Aslan and flung his arms as far as they would go round the huge neck; and he gave Aslan the strong kisses of a King, and Aslan gave him the wild kisses of a Lion. . . .

"But," said Eustace, looking at Aslan. "Hasn't he—er—died?"

"Yes," said the Lion in a very quiet voice, almost . . . as if he were laughing. "He has died. Most people have, you know. Even I have. There are very few who haven't. . . ."

C. S. Lewis
The Silver Chair

Prologue

The Door Slams Shut

The funeral service over, a small group of people emerge from the cool chapel into the blistering heat of a bright July day.

The grounds of the crematorium, like all such places, make an uninspired attempt at the creation of an earthly paradise garden.

The chief mourners are a strange quartet—two elderly men and two young boys. The men are brothers: Major W. H. Lewis and Professor C. S. Lewis. The boys, David and Douglas Gresham, are also brothers. Their four lives are bound together by the life and tragic death of an astonishing woman whom they all loved.

Born Helen Joy Davidman (but known to everyone as Joy), she was married first to William Gresham—father of David and Douglas—and then, for just four years, to C. S. Lewis.

The story of the love between C. S. Lewis and Joy Davidman is a curious one. At first glance, it seems hard to imagine two less likely lovers than they: Lewis, a sixty-year-old British bachelor don with a reputation for being the greatest Christian thinker, teacher, and writer of our time; and Joy, an American Jewish divorcée who had been a youthful member of the Communist party and who later became an adult convert to Christianity.

There is, however, no doubt at all that they were deeply, passionately in love. "We feasted on love," said Lewis, "every mode of it—solemn and merry, romantic and realistic, sometimes as dramatic as a thunderstorm, sometimes as comfortable and unemphatic as putting on your soft slippers."

Alone in his study, after the funeral, Lewis begins to confront the fact that this love, so lately won, is now lost to him forever.

Too tired to draw the curtains, he gazes at the reflection of his face, vignetted by night, in the window. A strong face with heavy features and round spectacles, it has, in repose, a look of resignation which might easily signify either peace or despair.

Opening an old unused manuscript book, he momentarily contemplates the arctic emptiness of the page, then takes his pen, and writes: "No one ever told me that grief felt so like fear . . . the same fluttering in the stomach, the same restlessness, the yawning. I keep on swallowing. . . ."

The bookcases on the walls around him are stacked with books, the kind of books to which a man might turn, in time of grief, for comfort, encouragement, or hope. To these books—such as *Miracles*, *Mere Christianity*, and *The Problem of Pain*—others have turned in their millions.

There they stand: volume upon volume, page after page, paragraph upon paragraph of insight and wisdom on matters of faith and belief, all of which are utterly useless to the man who wrote them.

Shipwrecked by grief, marooned on an island of doubts, Lewis finds his faith questioned, his convictions challenged, his beliefs assailed.

Where is God? Go to Him when your need is desperate, when all other help is in vain, and what do you find? A door slammed in your face, and a sound of bolting and double bolting on the inside. After that, silence. You might as well turn away. The longer you wait, the more emphatic the silence will become. There are no lights in the windows. It might be an empty house. Was it ever inhabited? It seems so once. . . .

Indeed, had not this man who now writes so despairingly once written about the inhabitant of that house with absolute conviction?

"Give up yourself, and you will find your real self. Lose life and you will save it." These were his very words.

Submit to death, death of your ambitions and favourite wishes every day, and death of your whole body in the end: Submit with every fibre of your being, and you will find eternal life. Keep *nothing* back. Nothing that you have not given away will ever really be yours.

Nothing that has not died will ever be raised from the dead.

Look for yourself, and you will find, in the long run, only hatred, loneliness, despair, rage, ruin and decay.

But look for Christ and you will find Him, and with Him everything else thrown in.

Why and how could such certainty turn to doubt?

In order to answer that question, we must first understand something of what made this man, and the woman he loved, the people they were. . . .

Through the
SHADOWLANDS

1

The Magician's Nephew

C. S. Lewis was born on November 29, 1898, the second son of Albert and Flora Lewis, in a semidetached house in Dundela Villas, near the outskirts of Belfast, Northern Ireland. His father was a solicitor and his mother the daughter of a clergyman.

He was christened Clive Staples Lewis, names wasted on one who, at the age of four, declared his name to be "Jacksie," and who was to be called Jack for the rest of his life.

A complacency about given names was evidently a family trait, since his elder brother Warren Hamilton was always known as Warnie.

Warnie was three years old when Jack was born and he later wrote of the event, "Of his arrival I remember nothing . . . it was only by degrees that I became dimly conscious of him as a vociferous disturber of my domestic peace."

However, as soon as Jack reached a more interesting age than babyhood, Warnie began to take rather more notice of his young brother. Before long they were devoted companions. "He never seemed to be an elder brother," Jack later recalled.

"We were allies, not to say confederates from the first." Warnie was to have equally happy memories of those childhood years, when they had laid "the foundations of an intimate friendship that was the greatest happiness of my life."

Jack and Warnie's parents were markedly different in temperament: their father, Welsh in origin, was sentimental and emotional, while their mother, of Norman stock, had a happy, equable disposition.

Jack later claimed that being aware of the contrast between his parents had bred in him "a certain distrust or dislike of emotion as something uncomfortable and embarrassing and even dangerous." It took almost sixty years for that distrust to be dispelled by a woman who, in a sense, combined the best qualities of both his parents.

The early years were highlighted by the annual seaside holidays at such romantically named places as Ballycastle, Castlerock, and Ballynahinch and regulated by what Lewis was later to call the "blessings" of his childhood: good food, good parents, and a garden in which to play.

The other blessings of his life were the family nurse, Lizzi Endicott (who awoke his young imagination with her tales of leprechauns and the old Irish gods), and his brother Warnie.

It was Warnie, Jack was later to recall, who first opened his eyes to the beauty of nature, when he

> brought into the nursery the lid of a biscuit tin which he had covered with moss and garnished with twigs and flowers so as to make a toy garden.... That was the first beauty I ever knew. It made me aware of nature as something cool, dewy, fresh, exuberant.... As long as I live my imagination of Paradise will retain something of my brother's toy garden.

Again and again in later years, Jack was to use the image of the garden in his writing, as a symbol of romance and mystery and life everlasting:

At the far end of one long lake which looked as blue as turquoise, they saw a smooth green hill. Its sides were as steep as the sides of a pyramid and round the very top of it ran a green wall: but above the wall rose the branches of trees whose leaves looked like silver and their fruit like gold. . . . So all of them passed in through the golden gates, into the delicious smell that blew towards them out of that garden and into the cool mixture of sunlight and shadow under the trees, walking on springy turf that was all dotted with white flowers. The first thing which struck everyone was that the place was far larger than it had seemed from outside. . . . Lucy looked hard at the garden and saw that it was not really a garden at all but a whole world, with its own rivers and woods and sea and mountains. . . .

In 1905, there came an important change in the Lewises' lives, when they moved to Little Lea, a new double-gabled house on the very edge of Belfast's suburbia.

Architecturally, it was a poorly designed house with frightful drafts, troublesome drains, and a warren of dark tunnels under the eaves leading to huge attic spaces. To Jack and Warnie, however, it seemed "less like a house than a city" and offered the prospect of unlimited adventures. From the windows in the attic, which Jack and Warnie quickly commandeered, they could look out across Belfast Lough toward the misty undulations of the Antrim Mountains.

They had little time to enjoy this new world together. A month after the move, Warnie was sent away to school in England.

Jack now began his own education, receiving lessons from a governess, but there was still plenty of time to be filled, although no brother to help him do so. "I am," he later wrote, "a product of long corridors, empty sunlit rooms, upstair indoor silences, attics explored in solitude, distant noises of gurgling cisterns and pipes, and the noise of wind under the tiles." He was later to re-create this attic world in his children's novel *The Magician's Nephew*.

The Lewises' house was crammed with books; they were to be found—sometimes two deep—in every room and on every landing. Some were suitable for a child to read; others were most decidedly not. Nothing, however, was forbidden him.

> In the seemingly endless rainy afternoons, I took volume after volume from the shelves. I had always the same certainty of finding a book that was new to me as a man who walks into a field has of finding a new blade of grass.

Most of the books he read were novels, biographies, and historical works (neither of his parents having much taste for poetry or romance). There was a lavishly illustrated edition of *Gulliver's Travels* and Mark Twain's Arthurian satire, *A Connecticut Yankee in King Arthur's Court*. There was also the *Strand Magazine* with monthly serializations: *Five Children—and It* and the rest of E. Nesbit's magical fantasies, and Conan Doyle's chivalric adventures of *Sir Nigel*, which awoke a passion in Jack for tales of knight-errantry.

The Tale of Squirrel Nutkin and other books by Beatrix Potter had already found their way into Jack's possession and had quickly caught his imagination with their natural settings and humanized animal characters. So taken was he with the idea of animals dressing and living like people that he began hunting through his father's collection of old *Punch* magazines in search of the elaborate animal cartoons drawn by Tenniel and others.

From these diverse sources would come, in later years, the inspiration for the talking squirrels, beavers, badgers, bears, and owls with which he populated Narnia.

Lewis once said of his children's stories: "I wrote the books I should have liked to read. That's always been my reason for writing." Doubtless the same reason unconsciously motivated his first attempts at storytelling.

Secretly written in the attic, Jack's earliest stories concerned an imaginary realm called Animal-Land, inspired by his chief interests at the time, dressed animals and knights in armor. "I wrote," he recalled, "about chivalrous mice and rabbits who rode out in complete mail to kill not giants but cats."

He also tried his hand at autobiography:

> Mamy is like most middle-aged ladys, stout, brown hair, spectaciles, kniting her chief industry etc etc. Papy of course is the master of the house, and a man in whom you can see the strong Lewis features, bad temper, very sensible, nice wen not in a temper. I am like most boys of 9 and I am like Papy, bad temper, thick lips, thin, and generally wearing a jersey.

Jack's solitary existence was punctuated by Warnie's school holidays when the brothers could share each other's company once more. On fine days they would ride off on their bicycles to explore the hills and lanes of the nearby countryside. When clouds lowered on the mountains like ghostly shrouds and rain fell in stairrods, they would retreat to their attic kingdom to draw pictures and write stories.

While Jack continued his saga of Animal-Land (and its rabbit-king, Benjamin VII), Warnie was composing stirring adventure stories set in India. Eventually the brothers decided to collaborate, and their two worlds were united by a series of detailed maps and historical chronologies.

When Warnie had to return to school, Jack simply returned to his books until the next holiday rolled around. This became the pattern of things for the next three years. Unbeknown to the boys, however, the ordered predictability of their lives was under threat. At the beginning of 1908, their mother was taken ill. It was cancer.

On February 15, Flora Lewis underwent surgery at home. Jack was aware that something was very wrong: "The house became full of strange smells and midnight noises and sinister whispered conversations."

27

Having been taught that prayers made in faith were always answered, Jack set about praying his mother better. He prayed, as he later put it, to a God whom he viewed "neither as saviour nor as judge, but merely as a magician." Nevertheless, his prayers appeared to be answered when his mother made an apparent recovery.

Then, within two months the pain and the cancer returned. In July, Warren was sent home from school before the end of the term because his mother's condition was worsening. Delirious and heavily drugged with morphine, Flora lingered on a month and then died on August 23, her husband's forty-fifth birthday. Jack and his brother were taken into the bedroom, on a day they would never forget, to view her body laid out in death.

Jack continued to pray, this time for a miracle, and when the miracle didn't happen, simply assumed that the magic hadn't worked. "I had approached God," confessed Lewis, "without love, without awe, even without fear."

Years later, when writing *The Magician's Nephew*, Lewis relived the pain of his mother's death through the boy Digory who is forced to choose between obeying the great Lion, Aslan, or obtaining the means to heal his dying mother. The setting is a children's story; the anguish is painfully real:

> "But please, please—won't you—can't you give me something that will cure Mother?" Up till then he had been looking at the Lion's great front feet and the huge claws on them; now, in his despair, he looked up at its face. What he saw surprised him as much as anything in his whole life. For the tawny face was bent down near his own and (wonder of wonders) great shining tears stood in the Lion's eyes. They were such big, bright tears compared with Digory's own, that for a moment he felt as if the Lion must really be sorrier about his Mother than he was himself.

In the story, Aslan gives Digory an enchanted apple that restores her to health. For young Jack there was no such happy ending. Separated from their mother, Jack and Warnie found themselves also cut off from their father by his inconsolable grief. The brothers "drew daily closer together—two frightened urchins huddled for warmth in a bleak world."

It took Jack a long time to come to terms with his mother's death:

> All settled happiness, all that was tranquil and reliable, disappeared from my life. There was to be much fun, many pleasures . . . but no more of the old security. It was sea and islands now; the great continent had sunk like Atlantis.

Fifty years later the specter of his mother's suffering returned to haunt Jack when Joy Davidman, the woman he loved, also lay dying of cancer.

In 1908, trauma followed trauma for Jack. Only a few weeks after his mother's death, he found himself being dressed in knickerbockers, heavy boots, an Eton collar, and a bowler hat, and packed off to England. His destination was Wynyard School in Watford, Hertfordshire, where his brother, Warnie, was already a pupil.

Lewis later referred to the school as "Belsen" and his two years there as "wasted and miserable." The headmaster, the Reverend Robert Capron (known to the boys as "Oldie") was a vicious disciplinarian who would mercilessly flog a boy for the slightest error in geometry.

Oldie had a number of favorite victims, and although Jack and Warnie were fortunate in not being part of that select group, they were nevertheless forced to watch the repeated brutalization of many of their fellows.

Despite the unremitting discipline at Wynyard, little seems to have been taught to the boys, apart from the meaning of fear. During the first year at the school, Jack wrote to his father: "We simply CANNOT wait in this hole till the end of the term," but the plea was ignored.

It was, perhaps, the all-pervading atmosphere of punishment and despair that sharpened Jack's response to the Anglo-Catholic services they had to attend twice each Sunday. For the first time he acquired a real understanding of the Christian doctrines and made a conscious effort to read the Bible and to pray every day.

If Jack found comfort in religion, he found escape in reading: books by E. Nesbit, A. E. W. Mason, Conan Doyle, Rider Haggard, and H. G. Wells whose science fiction stories were influencing Jack's early attempts at writing:

> "Bensin I'm going to Mars" he said in his short way. I laughed. "How?" said I. "In a vessel" said he "all I want is money." "Don't be a fool Brown" said I "you'll never do it!" "Oh yes I will" quoth he "at any rate I'll try." "It is wrong to commit suicide, specially when one has wife and children" I observed. "It is, very wrong" said Brown, "but I am not going to. However I thought I'd give you the chance of coming with me:—will you?" Come with him! I hadn't thought of *that*. I reflected and then said, "If you don't mind, Brown I'll wait till you have settled your arrangements." "Sorry Bensin" returned my friend "but I am going to start from central Africa, I sail from Southampton tomorrow night!"

There must have been times at Wynyard when Jack would have risked all the hazards involved in interplanetary travel to have escaped his educational concentration camp.

Release came in 1910, when the school was closed down and its headmaster certified insane. Warnie was now at Malvern College, but a new school had to be found for Jack.

Albert Lewis decided to enter Jack at the Belfast public school Campbell College, but his stay there was brief. After just half a term, Jack developed a cough that was bad enough to keep him away from school.

He recuperated at Little Lea in the company of a pile of books, while his father, who was for some reason dissatisfied with Campbell, made new plans for Jack's education, and enrolled him at Cherbourg, a preparatory school at Malvern.

Term began in January 1911, and Jack was able to travel to Malvern with Warnie, who was already studying at the college there. On arrival, Jack wrote enthusiastically to his father:

> Cherbourg is quite a nice place. There are 17 chaps here. There are three masters, Mr. Allen, Mr. Palmer and Mr. Jones, who is *very* fat.... Malvern is one of the nicest English towns I have seen yet. The hills are beautiful, but of course not as nice as ours.

Jack later claimed that it was at Cherbourg that his education had really begun. "I rapidly found my feet in Latin and English and even began to be looked on as a promising candidate for scholarship at the college."

Accompanying Jack's academic progress was a growing awareness that maturity—physical and intellectual—was a state to be highly desired. The onslaught of puberty found him easy prey for sexual temptation. The discovery that there were religious faiths that differed from his own—such as the pagan religions he read of in the classics, or the strange occult beliefs which the school matron introduced him to—caused Jack to abandon his own faith, "with no sense of loss but with the greatest relief."

Lewis was to look back on the changes he underwent at Cherbourg with considerable shame. Desiring "glitter, swagger, distinction" he said, he had worked hard to make himself "a fop, a cad, and a snob," and had succeeded.

But the pilgrim's regress was only partial. As Lewis wrote in his autobiography, *Surprised by Joy*: "Side by side with my loss of faith, of virtue, and of simplicity, something quite different was going on."

One day at school he happened upon the Christmas 1911 issue of the *Bookman*, which contained a colored supplement of Arthur Rackham's illustrations to *Siegfried and the Twilight of the Gods*. Leafing through Rackham's elemental paintings of heroes, dwarves, and dragons, Jack felt "the stab, the pang, the inconsolable longing" of an emotion which he later identified as "Joy."

Although he had never heard of Wagner or Siegfried, his mind was instantly filled with wild new images.

> Pure 'Northernness' engulfed me: a vision of huge, clear spaces hanging above the Atlantic in the endless twilight of Northern summer, remoteness, severity. . . .

A record magazine called *The Soundbox* provided Jack with synopses of Wagner's *Ring* cycle, and he at once began an epic poem of his own upon the same theme. Pocket money was saved up and spent on recordings of the *Ring*, *Lohengrin*, and *Parsifal*. Eventually, thanks to a seven-and-sixpenny half-share from Warnie, Jack was able to buy the cheap edition of Rackham's *Siegfried* and feast his eyes again and again on those dramatic illustrations with their brooding skies, knotted woods, and wizened earth men.

After Rackham and Wagner, Jack went on to devour everything else he could lay his hands on about Norse mythology. Such an obsession did it become that Lewis later speculated that if he could have found someone to teach him Old Norse, he would have jumped at the opportunity.

Perhaps it was as well he never had that opportunity or his other studies might have suffered. As it was, he lived up to his early academic promise and, at the end of the summer term of 1913, won a classical entrance scholarship to Malvern College.

By the time Jack enrolled at Malvern, his brother had already left. Having decided on a career in the army, Warnie was receiving private tuition from his father's former teacher, W. T. Kirkpatrick, at Great Bookham, Surrey, in preparation for his entrance exam to the Royal Military Academy at Sandhurst.

Jack viewed the prospect of following Warnie to the "Coll" with considerable excitement, and it is not surprising that his first impressions were favorable: there was the setting itself—noble buildings with castellated towers, cloistered corridors, and buttressed walls rising from broad lawns, dotted with ancient oaks; and there was also the "worldly pomp, power, and glory" of the school aristocracy, known as the Bloods. "The whole school was a great temple for the worship of these mortal gods; and no boy ever went there more prepared to worship them than I."

Still, Jack's time at Malvern proved somewhat less enjoyable. He quickly decided that Bloodery was a sham, potentially corrupt system. He was also irritated by the endless rules and regulations (official and unofficial), the floggings, and the requirement that younger students act as servants for the older boys. He was bored by the endless talk about games, which he was bad at, and the College Tarts (younger boys whom the Bloods took as lovers), which offered no excitement for him. Warnie wrote later,

> The fact is he should never have been sent to a public school at all. Already, at fourteen, his intelligence was such that he would have fitted in better among undergraduates than among schoolboys; and by his temperament he was bound to be a misfit, a heretic, an object of suspicion within the collective-minded and standardising Public School system.

One compensation was that Jack came under the civilizing influence of his form master, Harry Wakelyn Smith, affectionately known to his pupils as Smugy (pronounced "Smewgy").

> Large spectacles and a wide mouth . . . combined to give him a froglike expression, but nothing could be less froglike than his voice. He was honey-tongued. Every verse he read turned into music on his lips: something midway between speech

and song. It is not the only good way of reading verse, but it is the way to enchant boys. . . . He first taught me the right sensuality of poetry, how it should be savoured and mouthed in solitude.

During the year that he was at Malvern, when he wasn't shining shoes for the Bloods, Jack read widely. In class he was introduced to Virgil, Horace, and Euripides; in the school library he first encountered Milton and Yeats, and discovered a book on Celtic mythology that captured his imagination almost as powerfully as had the Norse legends.

For all the intellectual stimulation he received, Jack remained uncomfortable at Malvern and, at the end of his first year, begged his father to remove him. Somewhat surprisingly, Albert Lewis agreed.

He decided that Jack should follow in Warnie's footsteps and go to W. T. Kirkpatrick for private tutoring. Perhaps he was helped toward this decision by Warnie's success in his Sandhurst entrance exam—he placed twenty-first out of 201 candidates, and won a "prize cadetship."

About this time "another great good" came to Jack. Arthur Greeves, the son of the Lewises' nearest neighbor, had been ill, and Jack was invited to pay the convalescent a visit. The boys had been casual acquaintances, but nothing more, and Jack doubtless viewed the visit as more a duty than a pleasure. However, it turned out quite the contrary:

I found Arthur sitting up in bed. On the table beside him lay a copy of *Myths of the Norsemen.*
"Do *you* like that?" said I.
"Do *you* like that?" said he.
Next moment the book was in our hands, our heads were bent close together, we were pointing, quoting, talking—soon almost shouting—discovering in a torrent of questions that we liked not only the same thing, but the same parts of it and in the same way; that both knew the stab of Joy and that, for both, the arrow was shot from the North.

Arthur was soon to become, as Lewis later wrote, "after my brother, my oldest and most intimate friend." It was a friendship that was to last forty-nine years until Jack's death in 1963.

In 1914, Jack was so caught up in the Norse world of heroes and mighty warriors that he was only dimly aware of the international unrest that was growing within his own world. Warnie was on leave from Sandhurst when, on August 4, Britain declared war on Germany.

By September, Warnie had been appointed a second lieutenant in the RASC, and was soon heading for France with the British Expeditionary Force.

In the same month that Warnie received his commission, Jack traveled to England to meet his new teacher.

> He was over six feet tall, very shabbily dressed, lean as a rake, and immensely muscular. His wrinkled face seemed to consist entirely of muscles, so far as it was visible; for he wore mustache and side whiskers with a clean shaven chin like the Emperor Franz Joseph.

W. T. Kirkpatrick was, Lewis always maintained, the only man he had ever met who had come near to being "a purely logical entity." It was a quality with which he constantly challenged his young student, laying the foundation for Lewis's own incisively logical method of thinking.

Within two days of his arrival, Jack was wading through Homer for the first time. Kirkpatrick's methods of teaching were highly individual—offering the minimum of help, expecting the maximum of effort, but always giving enthusiastic encouragement—but to Jack it was "red beef and strong beer," and he wrote to Arthur Greeves that "after a week's trial, I have come to the conclusion that I am going to have the time of my life."

That is exactly what he had. The next two and a half years were of the greatest importance to Jack's intellectual development: "It is no sentiment but plainest fact to say that I owe him in the intellectual sphere as much as one human being can owe another."

To a boy steeped in the joys of reading, Kirkpatrick's house was a paradise. He read and translated Greek and Latin, but also found more and more new books to enjoy—Boswell, Spenser, Sterne, Malory, Morris, Ruskin, Keats, and Ibsen (even Virginia Woolf). The choice of what to read was limited only by Jack's literary curiosity, and that was virtually limitless.

One particular discovery, made at a station bookstall in nearby Leatherhead, was to have a lasting, deeply significant effect on Lewis, so much so that, when he came to write of it in *Surprised by Joy*, his description of the event was mystically poetic:

> The evening that I now speak of was in October. I and one porter had the long, timbered platform of Leatherhead station to ourselves. It was getting just dark enough for the smoke of an engine to glow red on the underside with the reflection of the furnace. The hills beyond Dorking Valley were of a blue so intense as to be nearly violet and the sky was green with frost. My ears tingled with the cold. . . . Turning to the bookstall, I picked out an Everyman in a dirty jacket, *Phantastes, a Faerie Romance* by George MacDonald. Then the train came in. I can still remember the voice of the porter calling out the village names, Saxon and sweet as a nut—"Bookham, Effingham, Horsley train." That evening I began to read my new book.

Years later, in his introduction to *George MacDonald: An Anthology*, Lewis recounted the same event, adding: "A few hours later I knew that I had crossed a great frontier."

Originally published in 1858, *Phantastes* is a beautiful—but disturbing—book, reflecting the deeply spiritual nature of its author who, before becoming a writer, was an ordained Congregational minister. George MacDonald's writing has a quality of passionate romanticism suffused with an enigmatic mysticism.

The book opens with an encounter between its hero, Anodos, and a strange fairy lady:

> "You shall find the way into Fairy-land to-morrow. Now look in my eyes."
> Eagerly I did so. They filled me with an unknown longing. I remembered somehow that my mother died when I was a baby. I looked deeper and deeper, till they spread around me like seas, and I sank in their waters. I forgot all the rest, till I found myself at the window, whose gloomy curtains were withdrawn, and where I stood gazing on a whole heaven of stars, small and sparkling in the moonlight. Below lay a sea, still as death, and hoary in the moon, sweeping into bays and around capes and island, away, away, I knew not whither. . . .

"That night," wrote Lewis of his first reading of *Phantastes*, "my imagination was, in a certain sense, baptised; the rest of me, not unnaturally, took longer."

He had been confirmed on December 6, 1914, merely to please his father, and took his first communion, as he later put it,

> in total disbelief, acting a part, eating and drinking my own condemnation. . . . It is true that I did not and could not then know the real nature of the thing I was doing: but I knew very well that I was acting a lie with the greatest possible solemnity.

Although Jack felt unable to tell his father his true feelings about religion, he was less restrained when writing to Arthur Greeves (surprisingly, since Arthur's family were Plymouth Brethren and he was a declared Christian). "All religions," he wrote in one letter, "that is all mythologies, to give them their proper name, are merely man's own invention." He now held agnostic views with as much conviction as he had once held Christian beliefs.

At Great Bookham, Jack continued to work hard at his studies, and Kirkpatrick was writing to Albert Lewis about his son in the most glowing terms:

> . . . it is the maturity and originality of his literary judgments which is so unusual and surprising. . . . He has read more classics in the time than any boy I ever had. . . . He is the most brilliant translator of Greek plays I have ever met.

Much discussion ensued about what career Jack should follow. His father suggested the law (which was his own profession), or the army (which was Warnie's), but Kirkpatrick had no doubts on the matter: Jack should go to the university. And the university, of course, meant Oxford.

2

The Myth That Really Happened

T his place has surpassed my wildest dreams," Jack wrote to his father. "I never saw anything so beautiful. . . ."

He had arrived in Oxford on December 4, 1916, a cold, frosty day, in order to sit for an examination for a classical scholarship. His visit began with something of a disappointment: on leaving the station, he mistakenly walked away from the town into the dull streets of the surrounding suburbs.

> Only when it became obvious that there was very little town left ahead of me, that I was, in fact, getting to open country, did I turn round and look. There, behind me, far away, never more beautiful since, was the fabled cluster of spires and towers. . . .

He retraced his steps and was soon overwhelmed by the architecture and atmosphere of what Keats had once called "the finest City in the World."

The day after his arrival in Oxford, Jack sat for his examination in the Hall of Oriel College. He later recalled,

> It was very cold, snow began to fall, turning pinnacles into wedding-cake decorations, and we all wrote in greatcoats and mufflers and wearing at least our left-hand glove. The Provost gave out the papers. I remember very little about them, but I had the impression that I was doing badly. . . .

Nathaniel Hawthorne once observed that "the world has not another place like Oxford: it is despair to see such a place and ever to leave it." When Jack left Oxford after the scholarship examinations, he had no particular expectation of returning there. He was convinced that he had failed. However, ten days later, in the list of scholarships published in the *London Times*, there was his name: "Clive S. Lewis, University College."

Founded in 1249, University is the oldest of all the Oxford colleges, numbering among its former students the poet Shelley. Although Jack was now a scholar at University he still had to pass the Oxford entrance examination, known as Responsions, which included a compulsory paper on elementary mathematics.

Since Jack found it virtually impossible to understand mathematics, however elementary, he was packed off back to Bookham for extra cramming from Kirkpatrick. From here he wrote excitedly to Warnie about the prospect of going to University: "Oxford is absolutely topping, and I am awfully bucked with it and longing to go. . . ."

There was, however, an obstacle that stood in the way of this happy anticipation: the war with Germany had now reached a critical phase, and conscription had been introduced in Britain. Although as an Irishman Jack was able to claim exemption, he clearly felt (with his brother already fighting in the front lines) that it was his duty to enlist as a volunteer. He discovered that passing his scholarship test would enable him to join the Officers Training Corps and possibly secure a commission.

As well as studying mathematics, Jack spent his time at Bookham reading (Italian and German, as well as English Literature) and writing prose and poetry that was mainly epic in length and romantic in style. He should, perhaps, have concentrated more on mathematics (and, in particular, on his weakest subject, algebra), since when, in March 1917, he sat Responsions, he failed the examination.

Despite this result, Jack was admitted as a scholar to the University so that he could enlist in the army via the University OTC.

Jack arrived at University College on April 26, 1917, and was soon writing long letters to Arthur Greeves that bubble over with excited descriptions of the place and its customs and inhabitants: there were the libraries and bookshops to be enthused over, and the unique delights of Oxford to be reveled in—such as boating on the river and visits to "Parson's Pleasure," a secluded spot where University men went for nude bathing.

Being at Shelley's old college made a particular impression on Jack, and he described for Arthur the poet's memorial, which he passed every day:

> On a slab of black marble, carved underneath with weeping muses, lies in white stone the nude figure of Shelley, as he was cast up by the sea—all tossed into curious attitudes with lovely ripples of muscle and strained limbs. . . .

In short, he found Oxford "absolutely ripping." He told Arthur,

> If only you saw the quad on these moonlit nights, with the long shadows lying half across the level, perfect grass and the tangle of spires and towers rising beyond in the dark. Oh ami, ami, what times we could have here together . . . what talks we could have in the privacy of these rooms by firelight while the kettle was boiling. . . .

41

Two months later, Jack was in "a Tommy's uniform," drafted into a cadet battalion billeted in Keble College. The realization that he would soon find himself taking part in a war which could well put an end to the delightful life he had just begun showed itself in his decision to gather together all his poetic writings in the hope of interesting a publisher:

> After that, if the fates decide to kill me at the front, I shall enjoy nine days of immortality while friends who know nothing about poetry imagine that I must have been a genius.

Although Jack settled down to his new life of military training, with its long hours of drilling and parading, he found it bitterly hard to give up what he had only so recently acquired. "You can't imagine," he told his father, "how I have grown to love Univ, especially since I left. . . ."

About his fellow cadets, Jack was scathing, seeing in them, no doubt, those characteristics he had so much come to dislike among his contemporaries at Malvern. Many of them he considered to be "cads and fools. . . . They don't need much description; some of them are vicious, some merely doltish, all vulgar and uninteresting."

There were, of course, exceptions, and Jack told Arthur that he had made "a number of excellent friends," including his roommate F. F. C. Moore, affectionately known as "Paddy," whom Jack described as "Quite a good fellow, tho' a little too childish and virtuous for 'common nature's daily food.'"

Paddy came from Bristol but his mother, Mrs. Janie King Moore (who had been separated from her husband for several years), was living in rooms in Oxford with her eleven-year-old daughter, Maureen. Paddy was soon taking Jack with him on visits to his family.

Mrs. Moore was an attractive woman of forty-five, with a strong, forceful personality. Jack liked her immediately. Liking, however, grew into a strange infatuation that was to have far-reaching effects. His closest friends—and even Warnie—were totally mystified.

In August Jack had three days' leave, which he spent with his father in Belfast, after which he was sent for a week's intensive training in Warwick. Then, on September 25, 1917, he was commissioned a second lieutenant with the Third Battalion of the Somerset Light Infantry. Jack was given a month's leave (an indication that he would soon be sent into action); this time, however, he chose to spend most of it with Paddy Moore and his mother in Bristol, going home to see his father for only a few days at the end of the month.

Jack's relationship with his father was at best an uncomfortable one. In *Surprised by Joy* Jack paints a portrait of him as an amiable eccentric:

> My father was no fool. He had even a streak of genius in him. At the same time he had . . . more power of confusing an issue or taking up a fact wrongly than any man I have ever known. . . . Tell him that a boy called Churchwood had caught a fieldmouse and kept it as a pet, and a year, or ten years later, he would ask you, "Did you ever hear what became of poor Chickweed who was so afraid of rats?"

To this whimsical habit was added an unshakable belief that "nothing was said or done from an obvious motive," as a result of which, Albert Lewis

> applied to the behaviour of people he had never seen the spectral and labyrinthine operation which he called "reading between the lines." Once embarked upon that, he might make his landfall anywhere in the wide world: and always with unshakable conviction.

The cumulative effect of these characteristics on Jack was to make him censor all his communications with his father—sometimes even to the extent of telling deliberate lies—in order to avoid needless confusion and misunderstanding. Now, and later, Jack was particularly secretive about his relationship with the Moores, and when, rightly or wrongly, Albert Lewis "read between the lines," this created a barrier between them that remained until his father's death.

Jack's friendship with Paddy, and his growing affection for his friend's mother, led Jack to make an uncharacteristically emotional pledge: were anything to happen to Paddy in the war, Jack promised to look after Mrs. Moore. Paddy probably made a reciprocal promise with regard to Mr. Lewis, but the burden of such a contract clearly lay more heavily on Jack.

His leave at an end, Jack was ordered to Crownhill, near Plymouth. A few days later, he was posted overseas. On November 15, 1917, he telegraphed his father: "Have arrived Bristol on 48 hours leave. Report Southampton Saturday. Can you come Bristol. If so meet at station." The address given for reply was Mrs. Moore's.

Albert Lewis, misunderstanding and confusing matters as always, replied: "Don't understand telegram. Please write." The next morning, Jack telegraphed again, making the message clear enough even for his father to understand: "Orders France. Reporting Southampton 4 pm Saturday. If coming wire immediately."

His father neither wired nor came. Jack left for France on November 17, arriving in the front-line trenches on his nineteenth birthday.

Early in 1918 he had, as he put it,

the good luck to fall sick with what the troops called 'trench fever' and the doctors PUO (Pyrexia, unknown origin) and was sent for a wholly delightful three weeks to hospital at Le Tréport.

Having learned from childhood "to make a minor illness one of the pleasures of life," he comforted himself with the satisfying thought that he had temporarily traded the trenches for a bed and the opportunity to do what he liked doing more than anything else—read. One of the books he read was a collection of essays by G. K. Chesterton, whose writings were later to have a powerful effect on Jack's thinking about Christianity. He was to reflect,

> In reading Chesterton, as in reading MacDonald, I did not know what I was letting myself in for. A young man who wishes to remain a sound Atheist cannot be too careful of his reading. There are traps everywhere—"Bibles laid open. Millions of surprises," as Herbert says, 'fine nets and stratagems.' God is, if I may say it, very unscrupulous.

At the end of February, Jack was discharged from the hospital and in the front lines once more. The war was now moving into its final desperate phase, and victory and defeat hung in the balance. Jack was to retain vivid memories of the horrors of trench warfare:

> The frights, the cold, the smell of HE, the horribly smashed men still moving like half-crushed beetles, the sitting or standing corpses, the landscape of sheer earth without a blade of grass, the boots worn day and night till they seemed to grow to your feet. . . . Familiarity both with the very old and very recent dead confirmed that view of corpses which had been formed the moment I saw my dead mother. I came to know and pity and reverence the ordinary man: particularly dear Sergeant Ayres, who was (I suppose) killed by the same shell that wounded me. . . .

That shell was not one of the enemy's, but an English one which fell and exploded in the wrong place on April 15, 1918, during the Battle of Arras. He wrote to his father a month later,

> I am doing exceedingly well. The wound under my arm is worse than a flesh wound, as the bit of metal which went in there is now in my chest . . . this however is nothing to worry

about, as it is doing no harm ... I am told that I can carry it about for the rest of my life without any evil results. ...

He concluded his letter with less happy news: "My friend Mrs. Moore is in great trouble—Paddy has been missing for over a month, and is almost certainly dead. ..."

By the end of May he was back in England, a patient at a hospital in London. Although the shrapnel in his chest was not causing any discomfort, he told Arthur: "Mrs. Moore and I are always hoping that it *will* start to give some trouble and thus secure me a longer illness. ..."

Clearly, Jack was now very attached to Mrs. Moore, no doubt finding in her the maternal affection he had missed ever since the death of his own mother; certainly her kindness and concern for Jack compensated for his father's continuing lack of interest. Although Jack repeatedly begged Albert Lewis to visit him, he never did.

Eventually, Jack was moved to a convalescent home near Clifton in Bristol (chosen so as to be near Mrs. Moore). A slow recovery from his wounds combined with the outbreak of an infectious disease at the home, which caused it to be isolated, prolonged Jack's convalescence, and prevented his return to France. On November 11, 1918, the Armistice was signed and the war was at an end.

Paddy Moore was now known to be dead. In a curious moment of charity, Albert Lewis wrote to express his sympathy. In reply Mrs. Moore told him:

> I just lived my life for my son, and it is very hard to go on now. ... Jack has been so good to me. My poor son asked him to look after me if he did not come back. He possesses for a boy of his age such a wonderful power of understanding and sympathy.

Jack kept his promise to Paddy and held himself responsible for looking after Mrs. Moore and Maureen. His brother and father were uneasy about this commitment, and about the fact that Jack was already giving Mrs. Moore sums of money out of his allowance. Albert Lewis thought Jack—"an impetuous kind-hearted creature"—was being taken in by Mrs. Moore, but Jack responded by refusing to discuss the matter and becoming increasingly secretive.

Jack was demobilized in December and, after a short visit to Belfast, returned to Oxford in January 1919.

> The place is looking more beautiful than ever in the wintry frost.... I arrived somewhat late in the evening. The moon was just rising; the Porter knew me at once and ushered me into the same old rooms. It was a great return, and something to be very thankful for....

He found that his war service had exempted him from having to retake Responsions, and he at once began studying for his Honor Mods examination.

Two months later saw the publication by Heinemann of Jack's first book, a collection of verse entitled *Spirits in Bondage*. "This little success," Jack wrote to his father, "gives me a pleasure which is perhaps childish, and yet akin to greater things...." The name on the title page was not C. S. Lewis but "Clive Hamilton"—a pseudonym derived from his own first name and his mother's maiden name.

One of the poems in *Spirits in Bondage* showed Jack's continued fascination with fairies, satyrs, tritons, and "a happy isle / where eternal gardens smile / And golden globes of fruit are seen / Twinkling thro' the orchards green...." It was a fascination that was to have its full flowering thirty years later in the Chronicles of Narnia.

In 1920, after working hard at his Greek and Latin, Jack sat for the Honor Mods examination, and received a First. In the summer of that year Mrs. Moore and her daughter, Maureen, moved to Oxford where she rented—with Jack—a house in Headington.

47

Following Jack's death in 1963, Warnie was to look back on his brother's relationship with Mrs. Moore, remarking that what puzzled him and Jack's friends

was Mrs. Moore's extreme unsuitability as a companion for him. She was a woman of very limited mind, and notably domineering and possessive by temperament. She cut down to a minimum his visits to his father, interfered constantly with his work, and imposed upon him a heavy burden of minor domestic tasks. In twenty years I never saw a book in her hands; her conversation was chiefly about herself, and was otherwise a matter of ill-informed dogmatism: her mind was of a type that he found barely tolerable elsewhere. . . .

In 1921 Jack made the first two visits to W. B. Yeats, then living in Oxford, remarking that he "could never have believed that he was so like his poetry." These meetings with the great Irish poet—now totally caught up in mysticism and the supernatural—were to shape one of the characters, appropriately a magician, in a long narrative poem entitled *Dymer*, which Jack began writing the following year.

> . . . He heard the noise of bees
> And saw, far off, in the blue shade between
> The windless elms, one walking on the green.
>
> It was a mighty man whose beardless face
> Beneath grey hair shone out so large and mild
> It made a sort of moonlight in the place.
> A dreamy desperation, wistful-wild,
> Showed in his glance, and gait: yet like a child,
> An Asian emperor's only child, was he
> With his grave looks and bright solemnity.
>
> And over him there hung the witching air,
> The wilful courtesy, of the days of old,
> The graces wherein idleness grows fair. . . .

The writing of *Dymer* and Jack's studying for Greats (the final examination for his B.A.) were carried on against what his brother was to call "the stifling tyranny" of Mrs. Moore. Of this tyranny, Jack himself good-naturedly recorded in his journal:

> It was unfortunate that . . . *Dymer* should coincide with a burst of marmalade making and spring-cleaning on Mrs. Moore's part. . . . I managed to get through a good deal of writing in the intervals of jobbing in the kitchen and doing messages in Headington. . . . I also kept my temper nearly all the time. Domestic drudgery is excellent as an alternative to idleness or to hateful thoughts—which is perhaps poor Mrs. Moore's reason for piling it on all the time; as an alternative to the work one is longing to do and able to do (*at that time* and heaven knows when again) it is maddening. No one's fault; the curse of Adam.

Despite many such interruptions, Jack took a First in Greats in 1922, and the following year a First in the English Schools as well as winning the Chancellor's Prize for an English essay. *Dymer* was finally completed and published (again under the pseudonym of "Clive Hamilton") three years later.

As the holder of three "Firsts," Jack was urged to study for a bachelor of literature or doctor of philosophy, but the need to support his adopted ménage made this impossible. His academic success had clearly made it reasonably easy for him to secure "a tolerable schoolmastering job," but Jack eventually decided to try instead for a fellowship in Oxford.

Oblivious to the fact that his son was sharing a home with Mrs. Moore, Albert Lewis agreed to continue Jack's allowance (which he increased from £67 to £85 a term) so that he could remain in residence until a suitable post became available.

Jack tried unsuccessfully for the fellowship in philosophy at Trinity College; then, after a difficult period during which he augmented his income by marking Higher School Certificates, he was offered the temporary appointment of philosophy tutor at University College while its holder worked in America for a year. The job brought him a much needed £200.

Jack applied for several other fellowships in philosophy, but remained unsuccessful. Then, in the spring of 1925, he tried for the fellowship in English language and literature at Magdalen College, "but without any serious hopes," he told his father, "as I believe much senior people are in for it." However, he was invited to dinner and various interviews, and, on May 20, was elected to the £500 a year post.

> "The President and Fellows of Magdalen College," announced the *Times*, two days later, "have elected to an official Fellowship in the College as Tutor in English Language and Literature, for five years as from next June 25, Mr. Clive Staples Lewis, MA (University College)."

Jack wrote telling his father the good news, his effusive tone belying the estrangement between them:

> First let me thank you from the bottom of my heart for the generous support, extended over six years, which alone has enabled me to hang on till this. . . . You have waited, not only without complaint but full of encouragement, while chance after chance slipped away and when the goal receded farthest from sight. Thank you again. It has been a nerve-racking business, and I have hardly yet had time to taste my good fortune with a deliberate homefelt relish. . . .

In October 1925, Jack moved into Magdalen College. It was to be his academic home for the next thirty years.

The following year he saw the publication of *Dymer*, which Arthur Quiller-Couch described as "a fine piece of work, fine in conception and full of brilliant lines and images. . . . He has that gift of metaphor too, which Aristotle was cunning enough to spot as the one quality of style which cannot be taught or imparted because it is genius, and its happy owner is born with it."

. . . Far in the dome to where his gaze was lost
The deepening roof shone clear as stones that lie
In-shore beneath pure seas. The aisles, that crossed
Like forests of white stone their arms on high,
Past pillar after pillar dragged his eye
In unobscured perspective, till the sight
Was weary. And there also was the light.

Throughout his postwar years in Oxford, Jack continued to read widely. His regular letters to Arthur Greeves contain much talk about a great diversity of authors, including Anthony Trollope, Algernon Blackwood, Sir Walter Scott, Thomas Carlyle, George Meredith, Ralph Waldo Emerson, and A. E. Housman, whose *A Shropshire Lad* he reread "for the hundredth time," describing it as "perfect and deadly. The beauty of the gorgon. . . ." He also read Chesterton's *The Everlasting Man* and concluded that its author was "the most sensible man alive—apart from his Christianity."

At Oxford, Jack had made several new friends and, as was his way, had thrown himself into working at these relationships: "I cannot quite understand," he once remarked, "why a man should wish to know more people than he can make real friends of."

One of the earliest of these real friends was Owen Barfield. Jack later wrote,

There is a sense in which Arthur and Barfield are the types of every man's First Friend and Second Friend. The first is the *alter ego*, the man who first reveals to you that you are not alone in the world by turning out (beyond hope) to share your most secret delights . . . he and you join like rain-drops on a window. But the Second Friend is the man who disagrees with you about everything. He is not so much the *alter ego* as the anti-self. . . . He has read all the right books but has got the wrong thing out of every one. It is as if he spoke your language but mispronounced it. How can he be so nearly right and yet, invariably, just not right? He is as fascinating (and infuriating) as a woman. . . .

51

What was distinctly curious about Jack's aptitude for choosing friends was that they either seemed to possess or acquire an interest in the religious and the spiritual—those very topics which Jack had purposefully repudiated. Arthur was already a Christian when Jack first met him and within three years of his meeting Owen Barfield, Jack's new friend had embraced anthroposophy, the theosophical teachings of Rudolf Steiner. Jack wrote in *Surprised by Joy*,

> Of course, it was all arrant nonsense. There was no danger of *my* being taken in. But then, the loneliness, the sense of being deserted . . . Barfield's conversion to Anthroposophy marked the beginning of what I can only describe as the Great War between him and me. . . . And this Great War was one of the turning points in my life.

There were other friends who were also to have a disturbing effect on Jack's smugly atheistic views: next was Nevill Coghill (later professor of English literature at Oxford and the author of the widely read modern English translation of *The Canterbury Tales*) who despite being "the most intelligent and best-informed" man in that class turned out to be "a Christian and a thoroughgoing supernaturalist."

Looking back on this period in his life with an amused relish, Jack wrote: "And so the great Angler played His fish and I never dreamed the hook was in my tongue."

Then along came Hugo Dyson, lecturer in English at Reading University and a frequent visitor to Oxford, and J. R. R. Tolkien, who in 1925 was elected professor of Anglo-Saxon at Oxford (and who later achieved worldwide celebrity as the author of *The Hobbit* and the Lord of the Rings). Both Dyson and Tolkien were Christians, the latter a Catholic.

His friendships, like many of the books he had been reading, were filled with traps for the unwary atheist. He was to later write,

All over the board, my pieces were in most disadvantageous positions. Soon I could no longer cherish even the illusion that the initiative lay with me. My Adversary began to make his final moves.

Jack began to review his feelings about "Joy." Of his first childhood experience of the emotion, he was to write, "It is an unsatisfied desire which is itself more desirable than any other satisfaction." It was, he had found, an elusive desire—hardly recognized before it was gone, leaving him wishing he were desiring it once more.

He had gone on to suppose that what he desired was Joy itself. Now he came to the conclusion that this was wrong: "All the value lay in that of which Joy was the desiring. . . . I did not yet ask. Who is the desired?" Jack was beginning to feel what Saint Augustine had experienced some 1,500 years before when he had written: "I loved not, yet I loved to love, and out of a deep-seated want, I hated myself for wanting not. . . ."

Gradually, almost imperceptibly, Jack was becoming a different person—or, rather, was becoming a *real* person:

> I felt as if I were a man of snow at long last beginning to melt. The melting was starting in my back—drip—drip and presently trickle—trickle. I rather disliked the feeling. . . .

Eventually Jack came to the conclusion that God existed, and then

> total surrender, the absolute leap in the dark were demanded. The reality with which no treaty can be made was upon me. The demand was not even "All or nothing" . . . the demand was simply "All."

So it was that Jack's Adversary made his final move. The chapter in *Surprised by Joy* in which Jack describes that move is entitled "Checkmate":

53

You must picture me alone in that room in Magdalen, night after night, feeling, whenever my mind lifted even for a second from my work, the steady, unrelenting approach of Him whom I so earnestly desired not to meet. That which I greatly feared had at last come upon me. . . .

Writing elsewhere of such a confrontation, Jack said:

There comes a moment when the children who have been playing at burglars hush suddenly; was that a real footstep in the hall? There comes a moment when people who have been dabbling in religion—man's search for God—suddenly draw back: Supposing we really found him? We never meant it to come to that. Worse still, supposing he had found us?

In the Trinity Term of 1929, Jack finally "gave in, and admitted that God was God, and knelt and prayed: perhaps, that night, the most dejected and reluctant convert in all England. . . ."

Jack's conversion was, however, only to theism, not to Christianity: "I knew nothing yet about the Incarnation. The God to whom I surrendered was sheerly non-human." The process which led him to an acceptance of the divinity of Christ was to take another two years and to involve two of his Oxford friends.

In September 1931, Jack wrote to Arthur telling him that he had a long talk with Hugo Dyson (who was staying as Jack's guest at Magdalen) and J. R. R. Tolkien. The conversation, which went on until four o'clock in the morning, began with "metaphor and myth" before moving on to Christianity. It was, said Jack, "a good long satisfying talk in which I learned a lot." The next two letters he wrote to Arthur were also concerned with this crucial conversation.

What Dyson and Tolkien showed me was that if I met the idea of sacrifice in a Pagan story I didn't mind it at all: again, that if I met the idea of a god sacrificing himself to himself I liked it very much and was mysteriously moved by it: again, that the idea of the dying and reviving god similarly moved me provided I met it anywhere *except* in the Gospels.

With Tolkien's help, Jack began to see Christianity in relation to the myths he already loved, began to believe that

> the story of Christ is simply a true myth: a myth working on us in the same way as the others, but with the tremendous difference that *it really happened*: and one must be content to accept it in the same way, remembering that it is God's myth where the others are men's myths: ie the Pagan stories are God expressing Himself through the minds of poets, using such images as He found there, while Christianity is God expressing Himself through what we call "real things."

Several years later, Tolkien was to develop this argument in his essay "On Fairy Stories" in which he defined the special quality of fairy stories as being the Consolation of the Happy Ending. This quality Tolkien called the *eucatastrophe* (the "good conclusion"). He wrote,

> The Gospels contain a fairy-story, or a story of a larger kind which embraces all the essence of fairy-stories. They contain many marvels—peculiarly artistic, beautiful, and moving: "Mythical" in their perfect, self-contained significance; and among the marvels is the greatest and most complete conceivable eucatastrophe.... The Birth of Christ is the eucatastrophe of Man's history. The Resurrection is the eucatastrophe of the story of the Incarnation. This story begins and ends in Joy.... There is no tale ever told that men would rather find was true, and none which so many sceptical men have accepted as true on its own merits.... To reject it leads either to sadness or to wrath.

This was the somewhat cerebral process by which Jack made his way to a belief in Christ. "I know very well when, but hardly how, the final step was taken," he was to write in his autobiography. It happened on a bright, sunny morning in 1931; Warnie and Jack visited Whipsnade Zoo, Jack traveling in the sidecar of Warnie's motorbike. Jack recalled,

> When we set out, I did not believe that Jesus Christ is the Son of God, and when we reached the zoo, I did. Yet I had not exactly spent the journey in thought. Nor in great emotion. . . . It was more like when a man, after long sleep, still lying motionless in bed, becomes aware that he is now awake. . . .

Remembering this day, thirty-five years later, Warnie was to write that Jack's conversion seemed

> no sudden plunge into a new life, but rather a slow steady convalescence from a deep-seated spiritual illness of long standing—an illness that had its origins in our childhood, in the dry husks of religion offered by the semipolitical churchgoing of Ulster, in the similar dull emptiness of compulsory church during our schooldays. . . .

In one of his letters to Arthur Greeves, Jack now wrote: "I have just passed on from believing in God to definitely believing in Christ—in Christianity."

Many years later, in his posthumously published book on prayer, *Letters to Malcolm,* Jack wrote:

> We may ignore, but we can nowhere evade, the presence of God. The world is crowded with Him. He walks everywhere *incognito*. And the *incognito* is not always hard to penetrate. The real labour is to remember, to attend. In fact, to come awake. . . .

He spoke from experience. In 1931, for the first time in his life, Jack Lewis had come awake.

3

The Middle-Aged Moralist

The time: Sunday, February 1, 1942. The place: a small BBC radio studio in Broadcasting House, London. A clumsy microphone stands on the green baize-covered table. The soundproofed wall clock shows the time as a little before 4:45 p.m. Sitting facing the microphone is a large thick-set man in a rather crumpled suit. His oval head is balding; he wears round spectacles and has a ruddy complexion and an honest, open expression. People who meet him for the first time are somewhat surprised by his appearance: he looks more like a country farmer than a distinguished man of letters.

The minute hand moves relentlessly toward fifteen minutes to five. The red studio light is switched on. The BBC announcer tells listeners that Mr. C. S. Lewis is about to give the third of five talks on "What Christians Believe." The green cue light flashes and the man at the microphone begins to speak.

For the next quarter of an hour he booms at the microphone in a voice that had been described as sounding like a cannonade at sea. He attacks the ether, bombards the listener with his thoughts and ideas:

> ... There suddenly turns up a man who goes about talking as if He was God. He claims to forgive sins. He says He has always existed. He says He is coming to judge the world at the end of time. Now let us get this clear. . . . I'm trying here to prevent anyone from saying the really silly thing that people often say about Him: "I'm ready to accept Jesus as a great moral teacher, but I don't accept His claim to be God." That's the one thing we mustn't say. A man who was merely a man and said the sort of things Jesus said wouldn't be a great moral teacher. He'd either be a lunatic—on a level with the man who says he's a poached egg—or else he'd be the Devil of Hell.
>
> You must make your choice. Either this man was, and is, the Son of God: or else a madman or something worse. You can shut Him up for a fool, you can spit at Him and kill Him as a demon; or you call fall at His feet and call him Lord and God. But don't let us come with any patronising nonsense about His being a great human teacher. He hasn't left that open to us. He didn't intend to.

These broadcasts, and the three books which followed (eventually collected as *Mere Christianity*), were a direct result of that spiritual struggle which had taken place in 1929, and which had brought Jack to his knees with the confession that "God was God."

The same year which saw the beginning of Jack's conversion also brought an end to the old life. On September 24, 1929, Albert Lewis died of cancer at the age of sixty-six. Despite Jack's differences with his father, he was deeply saddened by his death; he wrote to Warnie who was then serving with the army in Shanghai:

I always before condemned as sentimentalists or hypocrites the people whose view of the dead was so different from the view they held of the same people living. Now one finds out that it is a natural process. . . .

In one of several long, sad letters to his brother, Jack now wrote of their mutual feelings about their father:

How he filled a room. How hard it was to realise that physically he was not a big man. Our whole world is either direct or indirect testimony to the same fact. . . . The way we enjoyed going to Little Lea, and the way we hated it, and the way we enjoyed hating it; as you say, one can't grasp that *that* is over.

With his father's death, Jack's bond with Mrs. Moore grew even closer. In 1930, he bought a long, low, rather ugly house in the Oxford suburb of Headington Quarry. It was called "the Kilns" because there were some old furnaces—once used in brickmaking—standing in the grounds.

Jack, Mrs. Moore, and Maureen moved into the house in October. Two years later, when he retired from the army, Warnie moved in with them. Warnie was to spend his retirement in studying seventeenth-century French history—a subject about which he later wrote several books—and was soon adopted by Jack's Oxford circle. "The Kilns" was to be Jack's home for the next thirty-three years, and Warnie's until his death in 1973.

Jack found a new contentment at "the Kilns," writing to Arthur Greeves that he had discovered a feeling of "homeliness" and "connectedness," of being a part of the English country landscape. It was almost, he said, as if he were "growing into the soil."

He was also growing into his Oxford life—writing endlessly, reading extensively, and savoring his many friendships (that were to acquire even greater importance to him after his conversion). He pursued his academic duties with dedicated enthusiasm and, when he found particularly bright or receptive students, elevated the tutorial to the level of an intellectual partnership—though he was always, undeniably, the senior partner.

Some found him bombastic and thought that he held the average undergraduate in little more than contempt; others found his tutorials enlightening and invigorating, and relished the opportunity to join one of his evening sessions after Hall when the conversation (together with beer, port, or strong tea) flowed most freely.

Jack became a "character" about whom people were incapable of feeling indifference. He was liked and (far less frequently) disliked with equal passion. But he was universally respected, even by those who passionately disagreed with him.

Jack had little time for vanities: he set no store by possessions (not even books, which he would never buy if he could borrow them) or by his personal appearance (his suits were invariably in need of mending and pressing, and his shapeless porkpie hat was an Oxford landmark).

Perhaps because he had already seen so much of death, Jack held life as a highly valuable commodity, never to be wasted, always to be regarded as fleeting and therefore precious. Time was of the essence. His lectures—which unlike those of many of his colleagues were always crowded—were delivered at an exhausting pace.

He would frequently begin to speak in his booming voice (with much rolling of the r's) while on the stairs or in the corridor outside the lecture room. On entering he would borrow a watch from one of the students, speak digressively from carefully written text for precisely forty-five minutes, gather up his papers a few minutes before he finished, and stride from the room without waiting for questions.

Of his lectures during these years, those on the medieval tradition of allegorical love poetry were his most celebrated. In these he examined how poets such as Spenser in *The Faerie Queene* and Guillaume de Lorris in *The Romance of the Rose* employed the image of "courtly love." Despite his academic qualifications to write of such a subject, it was a curious one for a bachelor who had so assiduously avoided that emotion which men call "love," and who—apart from a few sexual encounters in his youth—had never embarked on a full relationship with a woman.

However, in his lectures on *The Romance of the Rose*—an allegory about a lover who seeks the beloved lady of his dreams within a beautiful and mysterious walled garden—Jack spoke with a depth of feeling that highlights, perhaps, his own lack of fulfillment:

> The dreamer in his wandering comes to a fountain. . . . Around it the grass grows thick and luscious, both winter and summer. In the bottom of the fountain there lie two crystal stones, in which the whole garden can be seen reflected. This is the mirror perilous and the well of love. . . . As soon as he looks into the crystals he sees in them, a little way off, a garden of roses, and among them one bud not yet unclosed. He is filled with longing for that bud; and turning away from the reflection he rises and approaches the rose garden to pluck the bud itself. . . . The Rose is clearly the Lady's love. . . .
>
> Descriptions of the act (or passion) of "falling in love" tend to be among the most banal passages of fiction; but Guillaume, with his crystals and his well, seems to me to give some of the real magic of eyes (and of mirrors) as that magic actually exists, not indeed outside the human mind, but outside any school of poetry. . . .

When, however, Jack published these lectures in 1936 as *The Allegory of Love*, the book was characteristically dedicated to one of his men friends: "To Owen Barfield, wisest and best of my unofficial teachers."

Jack's friends—particularly Owen Barfield, Nevill Coghill, A. C. Harwood, Hugo Dyson, and J. R. R. Tolkien—were very important to him for companionship, as an audience, as a source of intellectual stimulation, and, doubtless, as a means of escape from female-dominated life at the Kilns.

With some of these friends, he took walking holidays or expeditions, and they would frequently congregate in pubs or one another's rooms in order to drink ale, smoke their pipes, and engage in long discursive conversations on philosophy, religion, language, and literature.

It was this energetic group of intelligent men who were to form the nucleus of that informal club known as "the Inklings," which was itself a product of the friendship between Jack and Tolkien.

The two men had first met sometime around 1927, when Jack began attending meetings of another club which Tolkien had formed the year before. Called the Coalbiters, they met to read Icelandic literature in its native language. The name was derived from the Icelandic word *Kolbitar*, meaning those men who lie so close to the fire that they might almost eat the coals.

Although Jack could not speak Old Icelandic, he was an enthusiastic member of the Coalbiters, since the works which were read were part of that branch of literature he had so long loved. In the myths and sagas he glimpsed "Joy" once more—"cold, spacious, severe, remote. . . ."

Jack and Tolkien began to meet regularly together on Tuesday mornings, and the affectionate friendship that grew up between them was to provide a source of mutual encouragement to them both in their various literary endeavors. To Tolkien, for whom a difficult marriage and a large family presented many problems, it was especially important. "Friendship with Lewis," he wrote in his diary on one occasion, "compensates for much."

In the mid-1930s, both Jack and Tolkien became members of a literary society organized by an undergraduate at University College. Its members met to read their works aloud to one another and they called themselves "the Inklings"—a name derived from the word meaning a hint, whisper, or intimation (coupled, perhaps, with an allusion to the Inky Boys in *Struwwelpeter*, who were dipped in a giant inkwell as a punishment for bad behavior). "It was," said Tolkien, "a pleasantly ingenious pun in its way, suggesting people with vague or half-formed intimations and ideas plus those who dabble in ink."

The society did not survive long, but when it ended Jack retained the name and began applying it to their own gatherings. The Inklings would meet twice a week: on Tuesday mornings at the "Eagle and Child" public house in St. Giles, Oxford (always fondly referred to as the "Bird and Baby"), and on Thursday evenings in Lewis's rooms at Magdalen—remembered by most people as being rather shabby and very cold (though they did overlook the famous Deer Park).

The Inklings was initially comprised of Jack, Tolkien, and their immediate circle of academic friends, as well as Warnie; the Lewises' doctor, Humphrey Harvard; and Commander Jim Dundas-Grant, who had been in charge of the Oxford University Naval Division during the war.

In 1939, when the Inklings' meetings were approaching their zenith, they were joined by Charles Williams, who worked for the Oxford University Press and who was a prolific poet, critic, novelist, and theologian. Among Williams's books were *War in Heaven*, *The Place of the Lion*, *Descent into Hell*, and *All Hallow's Eve*, strange supernatural novels that he used to call his "spiritual shockers."

These religious fantasies were to have a dramatic influence on Jack's writing, and his relationship with Williams reached an intensity that all but eclipsed his earlier friendships, including that with Tolkien.

Recalling Williams after his untimely death in 1945, Jack was to remember his friend's face—sometimes like an angel, sometimes like a monkey—

> seen through clouds of tobacco smoke and above a pint mug, distorted into helpless laughter at some innocently broad buffoonery or eagerly stretched forward in the cut and parry of prolonged, fierce masculine argument. . . .

Others were gradually admitted to the Inklings, including Adam Fox, dean of divinity at Magdalen; Colin Hardie, classical tutor of Balliol and later Magdalen; and several younger men (some of them former students of Jack's) including Gervase Matthew, George Sayer, Lord David Cecil, Peter Bayley, Christopher Tolkien, and John Wain, who was to so vividly recall those meetings:

> I can see that room so clearly now, the electric fire pumping heat into the dank air, the faded screen that broke some of the keener draughts, the enamel beerjug on the table, the well-worn sofa and armchairs, and the men drifting in (those from distant colleges would be later), leaving overcoats and hats in any corner and coming over to warm their hands before finding a chair. There was no fixed etiquette, but the rudimentary honours would be done partly by Lewis and partly by his brother, W. H. Lewis, a man who stays in my memory as the most courteous I have ever met—not with mere politeness, but with a genial, self-forgetting considerateness that was as instinctive to him as breathing. Sometimes when the less vital members of the circle were in a big majority, the evening would fall flat; but the best of them were as good as anything I shall live to see. . . .

It was here Jack, Charles Williams, and the other Inklings read aloud from the books they were writing and listened to what must have been the best serialization ever heard, as week by week J. R. R. Tolkien would read them the latest chapter of his epic fantasy, the Lord of the Rings. It came, Jack said, "like lightning from a clear sky. . . ."

Parodying the opening of *Beowulf*, Tolkien wrote: "Hwæt! we Inclinga, on ærdagum searopancolra synttru gehierdon. . . ." Or "Lo! we have heard in the old days of the wisdom of the cunning-minded Inklings; how those wise ones sat together in their deliberations, skilfully reciting learning and song-craft, earnestly meditating. That was true joy!"

It is impossible to convey in just a few paragraphs the true substance of that joy, the depth and breadth of that wisdom, and the wit and invention of that song craft. Those who would know more about this unique literary group must read Humphrey Carpenter's excellent books: *J. R. R. Tolkien: A Biography* and *The Inklings: C. S. Lewis, J. R. R. Tolkien, Charles Williams and Their Friends*.

In 1933, two years after his conversion to Christianity, Jack wrote his first religious book, *The Pilgrim's Regress*. An allegory, loosely following the idea of a spiritual journey used by Bunyan in *The Pilgrim's Progress*, it is a partly biographical account of his own search for faith.

John, the pilgrim of the title, sets out on a long journey during which he encounters a great many characters including the Clevers and the Cruels, Mr. Sensible and Mr. Humanist, Mr. Enlightenment and Mother Kirk, as well as learning about the ways of the different places he passes, such as the Valley of Humiliation and the Cities of Thrill and Claptrap.

In a letter to Arthur Greeves (to whom the book was dedicated), Jack explained his purpose in writing *The Pilgrim's Regress*:

> I aim chiefly at being idiomatic and racy, basing myself on Malory, Bunyan and Morris, tho' without archaisms: and would usually prefer to use ten words, provided they are honest native words and idiomatically ordered, than one "literary word."

Clarity of thought and directness in communication were always Jack's primary aims in writing, and although he was to write many fine books of conventional apologetics—*The Problem of Pain*, *Miracles*, and the various volumes of "Broadcast Talks"—the allegorical form which he had experimented with in *The Pilgrim's Regress* was to remain one of his favorite ways of conveying ideas and beliefs.

In 1939, Jack published the first of three space romances, *Out of the Silent Planet*. As with the space stories he wrote when he was a boy, they were greatly influenced by the writings of H. G. Wells, although they are given an allegorical significance that is all his own. In adulthood, Jack found the majority of conventional science-fiction stories not at all to his taste and preferred the romantic fantasy writers—such as David Lindsay, Ray Bradbury, E. R. Eddison, Mervyn Peake, and Tolkien—to the work of social prophets like Huxley and Orwell or scientific visionaries like Arthur C. Clarke.

Out of the Silent Planet and its sequels *Perelandra* and *That Hideous Strength* place an earthman, Dr. Ransom, in the center of a cosmic arena where the eternal struggle between good and evil is being enacted. They are rich in exquisitely drawn symbolism while, at the same time, exciting and enjoyable adventures.

Stella Gibbons wrote that C. S. Lewis had created "a beautiful and dangerous world lit by hope." The enormity of his ideas and the compelling, totally believable settings for the stories make the Ransom trilogy not merely imaginative, but arresting and disturbing. More than that they are, as Sir Hugh Walpole remarked about the first of them, "a kind of poem."

> . . . He tried hard, in such stolen glances as the work allowed him, to make out something of the farther shore. A mass of something purple, so huge that he took it for a heather-covered mountain, was his first impression. . . . Beyond were strange upright shapes of whitish green; too jagged and irregular for buildings, too thin and steep for mountains. Beyond and above these again was the rose-coloured cloud-like mass . . . exquisitely beautiful in tint and shape. . . .

In the second book, *Perelandra*, the poem becomes a dance, a rhythm of ideas and words of which God—or, as he is known in the Venusian world, Maledil—is the origin and resolution. Ransom is told

> Where Maledil is there is the centre. . . . Because we are with Him, each of us is at the centre. It is not as in a city of the Darkened World where they say that each must live for all.

In His city all things are made for each. When He died in the Wounded World He died not for me, but for each man. If each man had been the only man made, He would have done no less. Each thing, from the single grain of Dust to the strongest eldil is the end and the final cause of all creation and the mirror in which the beam of His brightness comes to rest and so returns to Him. . . .

There were some among Jack's colleagues who thought Jack's foray into science fiction was regrettable and even indicative of a certain immaturity. Reviewers and critics were considerably less bothered by the fact that these astonishing books were the work of an Oxford don. Marjorie Nicholson said,

> Earlier writers have created new worlds from legend, from mythology, from fairy tale. Mr. Lewis has created *myth* itself, myth woven of desires and aspirations deep-seated in some, at least, of the human race. . . .

Whether the books would have reached as wide a readership, however, if Jack had not suddenly become such a well-known public figure, is a matter of some conjecture.

"It was the war," said Alistair Cooke, "that pitchforked Mr. Lewis into the limelight, for in doubting times completely unremarkable prophets are pressed into making a career of reassurance."

Is there any validity to this harsh denouncement, and was the prophet so unremarkable? When, in 1940, he published *The Problem of Pain*, one critic praised it for being written "with clarity and force, and out of much knowledge and experience," and no one could ever accuse Jack of failing to grasp the nettle:

> "If God were good," he begins, "He would wish to make His creatures perfectly happy, and if God were almighty He would be able to do what He wished. But the creatures are not happy.

Therefore God lacks either goodness, or power, or both." This is the problem of pain, in its simplest form. . . .

About one thing, Alistair Cooke was undoubtedly correct: it was the Second World War that made him into a household name. The invitation to speak on the BBC came from Dr. James W. Welch, the corporation's director of religious broadcasting, in February 1941. It was prompted by "the quality of thinking and depth of convictions" which Dr. Welch had found in *The Problem of Pain.*

In agreeing to give a series of talks, Jack said that he would like to speak on the subject of right and wrong, adding,

> I should mention Christianity only at the end, and would prefer not to unmask my battery till then. Some title like "The Art of being Shocked" Or "These Humans" would suit me. . . .

They were entitled *Right and Wrong: A Clue to the Meaning of the Universe?* and the fifteen-minute talks were broadcast live at 7:45 p.m. every Wednesday in August. The series was a huge success and Jack's clarity of thought and directness of speech soon established him as a radio pundit (rather as it had J. B. Priestley and C. E. M. Joad). He was, he used to say, just a middle-aged moralist.

Jack's newfound popularity had its drawbacks: "I had an enormous pile of letters from strangers," he told Arthur Greeves a few months later.

> One gets funny letters after broadcasting—some from lunatics who sign themselves 'Jehovah' or begin 'Dear Mr. Lewis, I was married at the age of 20 to a man I didn't love'—but many from serious inquirers whom it was a duty to answer fully. . . .

He added, in a postscript: "I'm giving 5 more BBC talks in Jan & Feb on Sunday afternoons. . . ."

This second series of talks was called *What Christians Believe*, a basic introduction to Christianity which included the memorably argued theory that it was impossible to deny Christ's claim to be divine and continue to think of Him as a great moral teacher. It was doubtless the popular style of these talks that irritated Alistair Cooke and others. The listeners, however, responded enthusiastically, and the published broadcasts sold well.

Becoming a radio personality had a dramatic effect on Jack's life, with countless invitations to speak and preach, and a lectureship with the RAF, traveling to the different bases and talking to the men about Christianity. Some of his friends thought Jack was receiving an excess of public acclaim: "Too much," commented Tolkien, "for his or any of our tastes."

It is somewhat ironic, therefore, that Jack should have decided to dedicate his next book to Tolkien, for it was to become an enormous best-seller and the most widely read of all his works.

The idea for the book had come to Jack in 1940 as he explained in a letter to his brother:

> After the service was over—one could wish these things came more seasonably—I was struck by an idea for a book which I think might be both useful and entertaining. It would be called "As one Devil to another" and would consist of letters from an elderly retired devil to a young devil who had just started work on his first "patient." The idea would be to give all the psychology of temptation from the other point of view. . . .

The Screwtape Letters, as they were eventually called, were serialized in the *Guardian* during 1941 and published in book form the following year.

The elderly devil was his Abysmal Sublimity Under Secretary Screwtape, who is employed in the Infernal Civil Service of Our Father Below. The letters are directed to his inexperienced (and rather inept) nephew, Wormwood.

Cunning—and, one might almost say, devilishly clever—
The Screwtape Letters have an effortless charm that conceals
the difficulty Jack found in writing them. "The strain," he
later wrote, "produced a sort of spiritual cramp. The world
into which I had to project myself while I spoke through
Screwtape was all dust, grit, thirst, and itch. Every trace of
beauty, freshness and geniality had to be excluded. It almost
smothered me before I was done."

> My dear Wormwood,
> I note with grave displeasure that your patient has become
> a Christian. Do not indulge the hope that you will escape
> the usual penalties. . . . In the meantime we must make the
> best of the situation. . . . One of our great allies at present
> is the Church itself. Do not misunderstand me. I do not
> mean the Church as we see her spread out through all time
> and space and rooted in eternity . . . fortunately it is quite
> invisible to these humans. All your patient sees is the half-
> finished, sham Gothic erection on the new building estate.
> When he goes inside, he sees the local grocer with rather
> an oily expression on his face bustling up to offer him one
> shiny little book containing a liturgy which neither of them
> understands and one shabby little book containing corrupt
> texts of a number of religious lyrics, mostly bad and in very
> small print. . . .

"Excellent," enthused the *Observer*, "hard-hitting, challenging, provoking. . . ." Charles Williams reviewed the book in the
form of a demonic letter from one Snigsozzle to a colleague
called Scorpuscle suggesting they should "make the infernal text
a primer in our own Training College. . . ," adding, "You will
send someone to see after Lewis?—some very clever fiend?"

Screwtape had his critics as well as his admirers. Years later,
Jack wrote to a friend with some amusement:

> Would you believe it; an American schoolgirl has been expelled
> from her school for having in her possession a copy of my

Screwtape. I asked my informant whether it was a Communist school, or a Fundamentalist school, or an RC school, and got the shattering answer, "No, it was a *select* school." That puts a chap in his place, doesn't it?

He also gleefully reported that his publisher had received at least one request for "C. S. Lewis's *Screwed-Up Letters.*"

With the publication of *Screwtape*, Jack's fame was assured; so too were the sales of whatever books he now wrote. Two further series of BBC talks were published as *Christian Behaviour* and *Beyond Personality*; and in 1945, Jack returned to the fantastic with *The Great Divorce*, in which he imagined what might happen if a busload of people were transported from hell to heaven and offered the opportunity of staying there.

In *Miracles*, published two years later, he made what he called "a preliminary study" of the miraculous, concluding that:

> God does not shake miracles into Nature at random as if from a pepper-caster. They come on great occasions: they are found at the great ganglions of history—not of political or social history, but of that spiritual history which cannot be fully known by men. If your own life does not happen to be near one of those great ganglions, how should you expect to see one? If we were heroic missionaries, apostles, or martyrs, it would be a different matter. But why you or I?

A few years later, however, Jack was to find a miracle—or something very like one—staring him in the face.

When Jack had begun giving talks on the radio, he had made it clear to the BBC that he would be holding his religious beliefs in reserve for a kind of final attack. When, eventually, he *did* reveal that what he had really been talking about was religion, he was quite unrepentant—although he did concede that some of his audience might be rather annoyed at finding that he had been "carefully wrapping up to look like philosophy what turns out to be one more 'religious jaw.'"

By now, Jack had discovered that he could, in fact, wrap up "religious jaw" as just about anything—even science fiction. Not that it was always a conscious or deliberate process—"I couldn't write in that way at all," he once said—but he had certainly found that fantasies and romances provided a medium uniquely suited to the expression of his ideas: "I wrote fairy tales because the Fairy Tale seemed the ideal form for the stuff I had to say."

Sometime in the late 1940s, Jack decided to write a children's book "in the tradition of E. Nesbit." It began, as had his three science-fiction books, with seeing pictures—and one particular picture—in his head:

> . . . a Faun carrying an umbrella and parcels in a snowy wood. This picture had been in my mind since I was about sixteen. Then one day, when I was about forty, I said to myself: "Let's try to make a story about it."

That story was *The Lion, the Witch and the Wardrobe*. It didn't begin as a specifically Christian story. "That element pushed itself in of its own accord" when "suddenly Aslan came bounding in. . . ." Aslan the great, beautiful (yet terrible) lord of the world he had created, became a symbol of Christ and the book an allegory of Christ's death and resurrection:

> Aslan stooped his golden head and licked her forehead. The warmth of his breath and a rich sort of smell that seemed to hang about his hair came over her.
>
> "Oh you're real, you're real! Oh Aslan?" cried Lucy, and both girls flung themselves upon him and covered him with kisses.
>
> "But what does it all mean?'" asked Susan.
>
> "It means," said Aslan, "that though the Witch knew the Deeper Magic, there is a magic deeper still which she did not know. Her knowledge goes back only to the dawn of time. But if she could have looked a little further back, into the stillness and the darkness before Time dawned, she would have read

there a different incantation. She would have known that when a willing victim who has committed no treachery was killed in a traitor's stead, Death itself would start working backwards. . . ."

Jack explained later,

I thought I saw how stories of this kind could steal past a certain inhibition which had paralysed much of my own religion in childhood. Why did one find it so hard to feel as one was told one ought to feel about God or about the sufferings of Christ? I thought the chief reason was that one was told one ought to. An obligation to feel can freeze feelings. And reverence itself did harm. The whole subject was associated with lowered voice; as if it were something medical. But supposing that by casting all these things into an imaginary world, stripping them of their stained glass and Sunday School associations, one could make them for the first time appear in their real potency? Could one not thus steal past those watchful dragons? I thought one could. . . .

When Jack had completed his story about four children who discover a magic wardrobe and, through it, find a way into the land of Narnia, he showed it to Tolkien, who was unimpressed. Feeling, perhaps, that Jack had aimed rather more at achieving an effect than at creating an Other World of the kind he was writing about in the Lord of the Rings, Tolkien told him that "It really won't do you know!"

Jack was discouraged and put the book to one side for a while before returning to it and rewriting the first few chapters. However, he still felt uncertain about whether it was any good or not, and decided to ask the advice of someone else.

Roger Lancelyn Green's first encounter with Jack had been when, as an undergraduate at Oxford, he had attended several of his lectures. He was now deputy librarian at Merton College and had recently published *Tellers of Tales*, the first of what were to be many books about children's literature and its authors.

73

One evening at Magdalen, Jack read Roger Green the first two chapters of *The Lion, the Witch and the Wardrobe* and, stopping suddenly, asked, "Do you think it's worth going on with?" Unhesitatingly, Roger told him that it was. He later recalled,

> As he read, there had crept over me a feeling of awe and excitement: not only that it was better than most children's books which were appearing at the time—but the conviction that I was listening to the first reading of a great classic.

The first of what were eventually seven Chronicles of Narnia was published in 1950 and was at once successful, its readers accepting the imaginary world of Narnia with, as the poet Kathleen Raine put it, "a passion that testifies to its truth to some world of imagination we all share." Apart from one or two goddaughters, Jack had little contact with—and knew even less about—children, but perhaps the truth in his stories sprang from his memories of the secret world he had inhabited in his own childhood.

Like its successors, *The Lion, the Witch and the Wardrobe* was embellished with delicate, evocative illustrations by Pauline Baynes that contributed so much to the total creation that is Narnia. Miss Baynes, who was chosen by Jack because he liked the illustrations she had made in 1949 for Tolkien's *Farmer Giles of Ham*, was at first quite unaware of the book's allegorical dimension. How much it tells us about Jack that he never bothered to mention it to her and how much, too, that explains the success of the book and its sequels.

Here then was Jack Lewis, the middle-aged moralist, at the peak of his creative career. But what of the man behind the outwardly popular and successful facade?

John Wain (one of the later Inklings), writing a few months after Jack's death, was to remember him in this way:

> The outer self—brisk, challenging, argumentative, full of an overwhelming physical energy and confidence—covered an

inner self as tender and as well-hidden as a crab's. One simply never got near him. It was an easy matter to become an acquaintance, for he was gregarious and enjoyed matching his mind against all comers. And if he liked what he saw of you, it was easy to go further and become a friend. . . . But the territory was clearly marked. You were made free of a certain area—the scholarly, debating, skirmishing area which the whole world knew. Beyond that, there was a heavily protected inner self which no one ever saw. . . .

No one? There were, of course, Warnie and Arthur and the most intimate of Jack's friends, but in the end it was to be a woman—a Jewish convert to Christianity who came from America—who was to discover and reveal that tender, well-hidden inner self.

4

Forbidden Joy

C. S. Lewis had an impact on American religious thinking and indeed on the American religious imagination
which has been very rarely, if ever, equalled by any
other modern writer." This was the view of American scholar
Chad Walsh, who went on to say that Lewis "performed a
special mission with people who were slowly finding their
way towards some sort of Christian orthodoxy."

One American whose thinking and beliefs were changed
through reading C. S. Lewis's books was Joy Davidman; eventually, and quite unexpectedly, her readings resulted in the total
transformation of both their lives.

Helen Joy Davidman (known always and only as Joy) was
born in New York City on April 18, 1915. Like many of
her generation, Joy was the first of her family to be born in
America, her parents—both Jewish—having emigrated there
from Europe in the late 1800s. Her father had been born in

Poland, while her mother's family came from a small village near Odessa, in the Ukraine.

Joy's paternal grandparents were Orthodox Jews—it is said that her grandfather died of pneumonia contracted while preaching Judaism to the Gentiles on the streets of Manhattan's Lower East Side. It was just as well then that he didn't live to see his son, Joseph, abandon the Jewish faith and profess himself an atheist.

In 1909, Joseph Davidman married Jeanette Spivack, whose family had all but given up their hereditary faith for a kind of humanist morality, while continuing, nevertheless, to pay lip service to the traditions of Judaism.

One of the major attractions of America to the many Jewish families who migrated there around the turn of the century was the atmosphere of religious tolerance. Despite their constitutional right to worship as they pleased, the Jews were a minority group with customs that tended to set them apart from others. As a result, their children frequently modified or surrendered their faith in order to conform with the majority and achieve a better life-style for themselves.

Wrote Joy Davidman in 1951,

> I was a well-brought-up, right-thinking child of materialism. . . . By now there is a whole generation like me in the cities of America. I was an atheist and the daughter of an atheist; I assumed that science had disproved God, just as I assumed that science had proved that matter was indestructible. . . . Before my time an atheist had been essentially a *religious* man, one who had thought about God and thought hard, if not well. But my generation sucked in atheism with its canned milk. . . .

Joseph and Jeanette Davidman were hardworking and socially ambitious. Since they both had employment, the family escaped the worst hardships of the Depression years, although Joseph was careful with money to the point of stinginess.

Even when she was a high school student, Joy was given only twenty-five cents out of which she had to find her fares and her lunch money—anything (and there wasn't much) left over, her father insisted had to be saved.

Nevertheless, Joy had a secure, comfortable childhood, a good education, piano lessons (with her own "baby grand"), and regular vacations to New England, and—more ambitiously—to the West Coast, where the family visited British Columbia, California, Washington State, and the Grand Canyon.

Early on, the Davidmans left the Jewish ghetto in Manhattan and moved to the Bronx, where a few reminders of New York's rural past had managed to survive. "You could still find rabbit tracks in the snow," she later told a reporter on the *New York Post*, "and there was an old-fashioned orchard with blue creeping myrtle under the trees."

After a few years they moved again to the respectable middle-class district of Grand Concourse. Although too young at the time to realize just how fortunate she was, early memories of life in the crowded streets of Manhattan prompted her to write in 1949 that city life "for many kids" had meant "being raised in a room where you can't sit, stand or lie down." It was, she said, "no use saying a healthy human being must adjust to our society, if the conditions of society are crazy."

While free from deprivations of poverty, Joy's childhood was not without its problems. Joseph and Jeanette were excessively protective toward their daughter, largely because from her birth (which had been a difficult one) she was a delicate child prone to illness. Her mother coddled her, while her father imposed strict limitations on what she could and could not do. Joy later came to believe that this treatment had made her unduly sensitive not only about her own problems, but about those of others as well.

Her greatest difficulties, however, were in relating to her father who, while professing concern for Joy's welfare, showed her little genuine affection. Lacking any vestige of a sense of humor, Joseph Davidman was a demanding man who set exacting standards for Joy and her brother, Howard, who was four years her junior. A rigid disciplinarian, he made the children respond to commands given on a whistle and, when they were disobedient, punished them by holding them by the nape of the neck and repeatedly slapping them about the face.

As she grew up, Joy developed—to her father's disgust—a sharp mind and a cutting tongue. She began countering his physical attacks with verbal cleverness. Joy stored up cutting remarks, such as a quote from Dickens on the maltreatment by parents of their children, and at an appropriate moment would "whack father over the head with it."

Physical discipline, however, continued for many years. Howard was still receiving beatings until he left home for college, while Joy endured it until she was sixteen, when she suddenly retaliated by lashing out at her father and scratching his face with her fingernails. He never struck her again.

As a young child, Joy developed what was to be a lifelong love of animals. "I suppose friendship for animals," she once said, "is a form of sympathy for the underdog." One of her favorite haunts was the Bronx Zoo. Often she walked the ten miles there because she didn't have enough money for the fare. She had a particular affection for the foxes and wild dogs, which she would try to tame, succeeding in getting one particular fox to come to her and take a piece of chocolate from her teeth.

Her greatest love, however, was for the cats. (She kept the domestic variety all her life and, while in Hollywood, befriended the famous MGM lion.) On secret nocturnal visits, sometimes with Howard in tow, Joy would go to the zoo and coax the lions and other big cats to the bars of their cages where she could stroke and pet them.

At an early age, Joy (like C. S. Lewis) discovered the delights of reading. When she was eight, she came upon the books of George MacDonald and read not only his children's books—*At the Back of the North Wind, The Princess and the Goblin,* and *The Princess and Curdie*—but also his adult fairy tale, *Phantastes,* the book which several years before had made such a striking impression on Lewis. Writing of MacDonald's stories, Joy said:

> They are the only children's books I know that make goodness attractive. They developed in me a lifelong taste for fantasy, which led me years later to C. S. Lewis, who in turn led me to religion.

Joy's passion for books rapidly developed. By the time she was attending school she was reading at least a book a day, and sometimes more. Joy was nearsighted, and her prodigious appetite for reading undoubtedly worsened the condition to the extent that she required glasses by the time she was nine and, in later years, was forced to wear thicker and thicker lenses.

At school, Joy and her brother showed exceptional talent. Howard scored an IQ of 147, while Joy had one in excess of 150. Despite the children's exceptional intellectual abilities, Joseph Davidman gave them little praise or encouragement. He derisively told Howard that he didn't expect the boy to make much of himself, and later dismissed his son's ambition to train in medicine as being far beyond his capabilities. (Despite this lack of support, Howard Davidman did graduate from medical school and became a highly successful New York psychiatrist.)

Throughout her school life, Joy was dogged by ill health, though it scarcely hindered her academic progress. First there was a problem with a crooked spine that went undiagnosed for several years. When she was ten, she was absent from school for six months with scarlet fever and then for several more months with threatened anemia.

Two years later, Joy was found to be really anemic. She was ordered onto a diet of liver extract that resulted in her putting on a great deal of weight. It was a difficult time for Joy: her academic precocity placed her in a class at school where she was much younger than her classmates; the overprotective influence of her mother prevented her from having many close friendships with other girls; and her concern about her appearance—she was short, fat, and bespectacled—together with her father's dictatorial attitude, ruled out any possibility of boyfriends. Compared with her fellow students she was very unsophisticated, but being highly intelligent and well-read, she felt herself to be much superior to them. As a result, she was very lonely.

Recalling this period of her life in 1949, when she gave a series of interviews to the *New York Post* about her reasons for leaving the Communist Party, Joy said:

> You begin to see how bookish, over-precocious and arrogant I was? I honestly thought I was better than anyone else. What a perfect combination for the Communist Party!

Joy was well on the way to embracing communism when she graduated, at the age of fourteen, from Evander Childs High School and entered Hunter College in the Bronx.

Hunter College had been established in 1870 as a tuition-free college for women. In 1930, most of its students were from lower-middle-class families who lacked the necessary finances to send their daughters to fee-paying schools. Many of Joy's contemporaries were from homes hit by the onslaught of the Great Depression, and some lived in actual poverty, although it took Joy (who was "too interested in growing up") a little while to react to the sufferings and hardships around her. She had, however, "a growing uneasiness in the region where my conscience should have been."

At home, meanwhile, she was becoming more rebellious. There were arguments and disagreements, and Joy began to question the motivation behind the rules of behavior her father imposed on her, which she found increasingly restrictive. She even began to detect in his attitude a note of hypocrisy and viewed her parents as atheists who lacked the courage to shake off the shackles of religious ethics.

Joy told her parents that they were the kind of people

> who deny Moses but still hold to the 10 Commandments or who deny Christ and keep the Sermon on the Mount. Your ethical principles mean nothing except as they express the will of God. There is no materialistic basis for ethics. If there is no God, nothing is wrong.

Pleasure, Joy announced, was the only real goal in life, and hedonism the only religion. Her parents were shocked and tried even harder to keep her in check. Her schoolfellows responded to Joy's passionate declarations that she intended to live for pleasure and the frequent stories of her parents' repressiveness by nicknaming her "Forbidden Joy."

Joy's rebellion was, however, one of the mind and spirit, and she did little to put her new beliefs into practice. "I guess I was as well-behaved as the average girl," she said later, adding that she continued to hold doors open for her elders and give up her subway seat to others.

Despite her stinging condemnation of religion, an experience she had about this time shows her to have been acutely susceptible to the numinous:

> When I was fourteen I went walking in the park on a Sunday afternoon, in clean, cold, luminous air. The trees tinkled with sleet; the city noises were muffled by the snow. Winter sunset, with a line of young maples sheathed in ice between me and the sun—as I looked up they burned unimaginably golden—burned and were not consumed. I heard the voice in the burning tree; the meaning of all things was revealed and the sacrament at the heart of all beauty lay bare; time and space fell away, and for a moment the world was only a door swinging ajar. Then the light faded, the cold stung my toes, and I went home reflecting that I had had another aesthetic experience. . . .

Although this and similar experiences which Joy had were in tune with those she had read of in the writings of George MacDonald and others, she resolutely refused to acknowledge them as spiritual.

> What happened to me was easily explained away; it was "only nerves" or "only glands." As soon as I discovered Freud, it became "only sex." And yet if ever a human life was haunted, Christ haunted me.

Religious symbolism was an integral part of much of the literature she had read: it was in MacDonald, in the stories of Lord Dunsany and William Morris and the work of the mystical poets whom she read, from John Donne to Francis Thompson. There was also the Bible which Joy had read "for its literary beauty, of course!" These influences had a curious effect:

> I quoted Jesus unconsciously in everything I did, from writing verse to fighting my parents. My first published poem was called "Resurrection"—a sort of private argument with Jesus, attempting to convince him (and myself) that he had never risen. I wrote it at Easter, of all possible seasons, and never guessed why.

Christ and His Passion became a recurrent theme in the poetry that she had been writing ever since her discovery of Keats and Shelley had led her to a career as a poet. Yet, she confessed years afterward, Jesus was little more than "a valuable literary convention." Though she might be "seized and shaken by spiritual powers a dozen times a day," she still succeeded in taking it for granted that there was no such thing as spirit.
In 1930, she believed in nothing:

> Men, I said, were only apes. Virtue is only custom. Life is only an electrochemical reaction. Mind is only a set of conditioned reflexes. . . . Love, art, and altruism are only sex. The universe

is only matter. Matter is only energy. I forget what I said energy only was. . . .

And so the young Joy developed and refined her image of being a happy materialist:

In the greedy, grabbing, big-city, middle-class world I knew, this seemed the sort of person that was wanted. But underneath the surface my own real personality stirred, stretched its wings, discovered its own tastes. . . .

At Hunter College, Joy worked hard at her studies and continued to write. She was one of the editors of the *Hunter College Echo* and published there a short story entitled "Apostate." The story tells of a young Jewish girl in Russia who elopes with a Christian and agrees to be baptized in order to marry him. But the baptism ceremony never takes place: her family arrive and mercilessly beat her, while the Christians look on and laugh. "Apostate" was awarded the Bernard Cohen Short Story Prize in 1934.

Later that year, Joy graduated from Hunter with a B.A. and, following postgraduate studies for an M.A. at Columbia University, she became a teacher. "I was," she later said with some pride, "sensationally not a success!"

Joy disliked teaching—it was her parents' idea, not hers; she still wanted to be a writer, but teaching used all her available physical and intellectual energy and left little time for writing.

She was teaching English at Walton High School when, in 1935, she became seriously ill. Joy, who was twenty, was found to be suffering from Graves' disease—an overactivity of the thyroid which caused a goiter around her neck, protruding eyes, and chronic weariness. At first, surgery was proposed, in order to remove part of the thyroid; then it was suggested that, instead, she should receive radium treatment.

Once a week, for the next year, Joy wore a radium belt around her neck for twenty-four hours. The radium, it was argued, would be absorbed by the thyroid and would reduce its activity. The disease responded to the treatment, but the sustained exposure to radium doubtless contributed to the cancer from which she suffered twenty years later.

Eventually, Joy returned to teaching, this time at Roosevelt High School. Here the work was harder and even less rewarding than it had been at her previous school. The students, many of them Italian-Americans with next to no English, came from some of the poorest, most downtrodden families in New York.

Many of the teachers were experiencing hardship as well, since the school authorities operated a money-saving system under which teachers were employed as "permanent substitutes" (sometimes for as long as ten years) on salaries that were far lower than those of established teachers. Additionally, these substitutes were required to carry out a variety of non-teaching chores ranging from typing to scrubbing classroom floors. Joy began to sense and identify with a deep dissatisfaction over the state of American society.

The horrific reality of life in Depression America had first hit Joy a few months before her graduation from Hunter. She had been looking out of the window at college one day, when she saw a girl standing precariously on the roof of an adjacent wing. Before Joy had had time to do more than wonder what the girl was doing there, she had jumped to her death. Joy later discovered that the girl was an orphan living on social relief and, when her check had failed to arrive, had gone for several days without food. Lonely and despairing, the girl had finally decided that suicide was the only way out.

Joy was moved and angered by the experience and, during the next few years, became increasingly aware that the suicide of this unknown girl was no isolated occurrence. New York was rife with suffering and hardship. Honest men who had always been hardworking were unemployed and destitute;

people were forced to abandon their pride and stand in bread lines or steal from garbage cans.

At the same time, elsewhere on the continent, crops of which there was a glut were being wantonly destroyed. It is scarcely surprising that in their anger, hunger, and penury, some Americans began to turn to an alternative political philosophy—communism.

At Roosevelt High School, as in a number of other New York schools, several teachers joined the Communist party.

Increasingly, Joy found herself brooding on social and political issues she had never really considered before. One day, while on a long walk, she was debating these issues in her mind, when she suddenly stopped short. "If I keep on thinking like this," she told herself, "I'll be a Communist." Then, to her astonishment, she added, "By God, I *am* a Communist!"

Abandoning the blind patriotism of her parents' generation, Joy began to think, and write, about what she saw as a far higher sentiment: the love, not of nation, but of the people it comprised—the people suffering under the inequalities of capitalism:

> Break a wheatstraw and bring it home,
> This is your share of America,
> The earth is possessed and used evilly. . . .
> Break a stalk of cactus and take it home with you
> and do not question why the thorns cause you pain;
> this is what you are given out of the plain.
> Now with me bow down and love this earth
> which you have not had for your own; touch it with your
>   forehead.
> Repair its wounds with the piety of your fingers.
> You will make it a fine earth belonging to its people. . . .
> Now with me
> bow and set your mouth against America
> which you will make fine and the treasure of its men,
> which you will give to the workers and to those who turn
>   land over with the plow.

There were other influences at work, helping to move Joy nearer to a communist standpoint. First there was an artistic influence as Joy began to discover the work of Soviet writers, musicians, and filmmakers: "There couldn't," she argued, "be much wrong with a country able to produce pictures so superior to most of those being produced here." Then there were the daily news reports of the civil war in Spain where many Americans, together with volunteers from other countries, were helping the left-wing Republicans fight against the fascist army of General Franco.

The strongest influence, however, was one which Joy only recognized many years later:

> Most of all, I think I was moved by the same unseen power that had directed my reading and my dreaming—I became a communist because, later on, I was going to become a Christian.

For years, Joy had preached the selfish creed of hedonism; now, for the first time in her life, she wanted to be involved with the problems of others—"I was willing to be my brother's keeper." It was an instinctive, emotional response: Joy made no effort to study Marxism; it was enough that capitalism had failed and socialism was offering the world a viable alternative. She later wrote,

> My motives were a mixed lot. Youthful rebelliousness, youthful vanity, youthful contempt of the "stupid people" who seemed to be running society, all these played a part. The world was out of joint, and goody, goody, who so fit as I to set it right? Maybe no rational person would worry about the rest of the world; I found myself worrying all the same. And I wanted to *do* something, so I joined the Communist Party.

She called on a former classmate of hers from Hunter College, who lived in the Bronx and who had become a communist. Joy had expected to be welcomed with open arms, but her friend was rather cool, recommending Joy read some literature on the party and saying that she would then discuss it with her further.

A few days later, having read a couple of pamphlets on communism, Joy met with her friend again:

> That very evening a note of warning was struck of the thing that eventually was to drive me out of the Party. . . . I was excitedly telling of my change of heart, when my friend said suspiciously: "Do you want to come in to help other people?" A good deal of natural rebelliousness was concealed behind my decision, but I did want to help other people. Something warned me "yes" would be the wrong answer.
>
> Then and there I told my first lie for the Party. . . . "To hell with other people!" I declared. "I want to join the communists for my own sake, because I know I can't have a decent future without socialism!"
>
> That was the right answer. . . . My friend relaxed and smiled. My Marxist education, the process of getting rid of my "bourgeois values," had begun.

Her concern and compassion for humanity, however, remained as strong as ever, and although she may have succeeded in concealing this from her communist friends, it continued to shine through her poetry:

> When war and ruined men shall cease
> To vex my body's house of peace,
> And bloody children lying dead
> Let me lie softly in my bed
> To nurse a whole and sacred skin,
> Break roof and let the bomb come in. . . .
> Let me have eyes I need not shut;
> Let me have truth at my tongue's root;
> Let courage and the brain command
> The honest fingers of my hand;
> And when I wait to save my skin
> Break roof and let my death come in.

Although Joy had found it relatively easy to declare her allegiance to communism, she found it anything but easy to become a party member. First at a branch meeting, then at a large rally in Madison Square Garden, Joy took the oath to Marx and the working class, but on neither occasion did it lead to the issuing of a party card.

Undaunted, Joy tried yet again, this time when a young man (who was a party member) took her to a meeting on lower Fifth Avenue. Here Joy was finally sworn in and given her card and dues book. Her parents, when she told them, were deeply shocked; but despite rows with her father on the subject, Joy stuck by her convictions. Because it was "the thing to do," Joy took a party name, calling herself "Nell Thulchin."

Thulchin was the name of the small Ukrainian village where her mother had lived as a child and the setting for Joy's first novel, *Anya*, which she was now writing.

Joy had resigned her teaching post in the summer of 1937, and with the support—rather surprisingly—of her parents, began seriously pursuing her ambition to write.

Based on incidents and people from the reminiscences of her mother, *Anya* is a moving portrait of a young Jewess growing up in Russia and of the men she loved. It is a story of the Old World, steeped in the language and customs of the past, but told with the style and perception of a child of the New World. It is a long novel—almost 300 pages—but it is written with pace and economy and richly evocative observation of time and place:

> . . . It was a country of silver straw and pale gold, except for the late cornflowers here and there standing dark above the ground. Near at hand each blade of stubble was distinct and jagged, throwing off its own glint of broken sunlight; but the fields grew insubstantial in the distance. . . . Anya walked along the road out of the town, stopping now and then to press her hands against the stubble and feel it prick her. She was twelve years old and a child of the Jewish quarter of Shpikov.

The great airy emptiness of the fields seemed to take her by the throat.

Anya herself is a woman of passion and sensuality, observing and yet struggling against the traditions of her people. At the end of the novel, about to bear the child of a man who is not her husband, Anya dreams of a new life in America:

> ...Her mind curled itself lovingly around the thought of that country, touching the gold that was everywhere in its streets; walking in pride among the foreign shining houses. America was a new life, the taste of a new drink, the touch of a new man on her shoulder.... In America there were spiced things to eat; cakes with a shine on them, and silks with a shine, and men with foreign, unexpected eyes to look at a woman in the street. Thinking this, she remembered that she was an old woman and was assailed by a sharp memory of Shimka. But she tasted her recollection of him with pleasure, she could not make it hurt her; the seven months she had spent with him were a closed part of her life; his place was taken in her love by the teasing, sweet, adventurous promise of America....

We are not told whether Anya finally realizes her dreams and reaches America, but we are left in little doubt that, if and when she does, she will find things very different from what she expects. Nevertheless, *Anya* is not a political novel and contains no particular indication of Joy's newfound ideologies. For that one must look to her poetry.

During 1936 and 1937, several of Joy's poems were published by the highly prestigious magazine *Poetry*, while others—containing anguished cries about war, poverty, and the picket line—appeared in the semi-official Communist party magazine, *New Masses*. Encouraged by these successes, Joy decided to submit her work to the distinguished writer, Stephen Vincent Benét, who edited the Yale University Press's "Younger Poet Series," the aim of which was to publish "such verse as seems to give the fairest promise for the future of American poetry." Competition for a place in the series—which already included Oscar Williams and James Agee—was intense.

Benét detected in Joy's poetry "very considerable command of technique and an individuality that can express itself successfully in a variety of forms" and decided to publish forty-five of the poems submitted.

In his introduction to the book, published in November 1938, Benét wrote:

> Here is what an intelligent, sensitive, and vivid mind thinks about itself and the things of the modern world. Because of her power, her vividness, and her sharp expression of much that is felt and thought by many of her generation, I hope that Miss Davidman's book will reach a rather larger audience than that generally reserved for first books of verse.

The book took its title from its opening poem—*Letter to a Comrade*:

> ... Say then to these, there is no miracle of help
> fixed in the stars, there is no magic, no saviour
> smiling in blatant ink on election posters;
> only the strength of men, only the twigs bound together
> invent the faggot, only the eyes that go seeking
> find help in brothers eyes. Say only
> the spirit of men builds bridges of the spirit,
> the hands of men contrive united splendours,
> the needs of men shall awaken thunderous answers. . . .

5

And God Came In

The trouble with most of the poetically inspired comrades was that they thought all you had to do to create a poem was chop a *Daily Worker* editorial into free verse. . . ."

This was how Joy Davidman was to reflect on the poetry of communism. She was in a good position to make such a judgment, having for some years occupied the unpaid post of poetry reader for the Communist party publication *New Masses*. "I must have been devoted," she wrote later, "because the stuff submitted was generally pretty awful."

Her own poetry, however, was in a very different class. *Letter to a Comrade* collected excellent reviews—one critic praising its "plasticity of technique, clarity of image, affirmative strength and flexibility of thought"—and quickly sold out its first printing.

The book was reprinted in the spring of 1939, and that year won the Russell Loines Award of the National Institute of Arts and Letters. The prize was $1,000, but even more important to Joy was that she won the award jointly with the poetry-genius of New England, Robert Frost.

Although Joy was signed on as a client of one of New York's leading literary agents, Brandt and Brandt, she decided that her talents should primarily be employed in the service of the communist cause, and her willingness to write for the party led the editor of *New Masses* to promote her from poetry reader to journalist and critic.

But, for all her protestations of zeal, Joy did not fit comfortably into the Communist party milieu. She found her colleagues dull, pompous, and lacking any sense of humor; many were also bereft of talent: "One reason some of them were there may have been they were incompetent to hold down decent jobs elsewhere."

Joy took up knitting to while away the boring editorial meetings, though she often dropped her stitches when discussions reached a level that finally prompted her to make a stormy intervention. She caustically informed the editors that the only reason party members bought communist publications was out of duty "since nobody could possibly pretend that they were interesting."

On one occasion Joy said in an editorial meeting that *New Masses* was badly in need of "a little literary polish." Her colleagues looked aghast. "What! Do you want us to be like the *New Yorker*?" they asked, to which Joy defiantly replied that she did.

With an award-winning book of verse to her credit and her first novel accepted for publication by Macmillan, it is hardly surprising that Joy considered herself superior to the bores and hacks with whom she worked. Nor is it at all surprising that, given the opportunity to do something other than write propagandist poetry for *New Masses*, Joy should have leapt at it.

The opportunity came when, in 1939, she was invited to go to Hollywood—that city of dreams once described as "a place where the inmates are in charge of the asylum."

In 1938, the Metro-Goldwyn-Mayer studio had launched a scheme to find new writing talent by inviting a number of promising young writers to try their hand at scripting movies. Contracts were initially for six months, and recipients were paid a guaranteed $50 a week.

Hollywood, with its palm-fringed sidewalks and palatial mansions, was a curious destination for a writer with an overactive social conscience, but the incentives were great: more money than she had ever received before; an opportunity to increase her experience; the chance that this might be the beginning of a new career; and a highly desirable period of freedom away from home.

Joy arrived in Hollywood in April 1939. It happened, by chance, to be one of MGM's most triumphant years. Among the fifty-two pictures released (one for every week of the year) were several big successes: Robert Donat in *Goodbye, Mr. Chips*; Mickey Rooney in *The Adventures of Huckleberry Finn*; Greta Garbo in *Ninotchka*; Judy Garland and friends in *The Wizard of Oz*; and one of the greatest movie blockbusters of all time—*Gone With the Wind*.

For Joy, however, it was to be a singularly unsuccessful time. Unlike some of the other writers who migrated to Hollywood—such as James Hilton, Anita Loos, and R. C. Sherriff—Joy Davidman failed to come to grips with the very particular skills required of the screenwriter.

Although she wrote at least four scripts, none of them was ever used. One of the screenplays on which she worked was *Rage in Heaven*, a melodrama eventually filmed in 1941 with Robert Montgomery, Ingrid Bergman, and George Sanders. The final script was written by Christopher Isherwood, although not before James Hilton had tried his hand at a version. On its release, Joy reviewed *Rage in Heaven*, confessing: "This writer had a crack at writing it, too, in her Metro-Goldwyn-Mayer days, and it is with great magnanimity that she admits the film is much better than she or James Hilton left it."

At the time, however, she was deeply disappointed, failing to appreciate that her failure may well have had less to do with her personal abilities than with the Hollywood studio system, where scripts were frequently passed from writer to writer before a screenplay was produced that satisfied the producers.

Looking back on this period of MGM movies, Louis B. Mayer was to say: "I wanted warm stories, sentimental entertainment. Sophisticates call that corn. All right, so it's corn. What's wrong with corn? It's only when rough, crude people put out corn that it becomes corny." In view of this criterion, it is hardly to be wondered at that such a serious-minded writer as Joy failed to deliver the right kind of scripts.

Joy, not unnaturally perhaps, blamed Hollywood for failing to appreciate her talents. Rather unwisely, however, she openly mocked the movie industry, agreeing with Oscar Levant's observation that "Behind the phony tinsel of Hollywood lies the real tinsel." The industry—and in particular the bosses at MGM—was not amused by the egotism of a $50 a week writer who hadn't managed to come up with a filmable script.

Instead of joining the Hollywood party circuit, Joy spent her evenings at Communist party meetings. The only friends she seems to have made were a man with whom she had a half-hearted affair, and Leo—the MGM lion.

In the autumn, Joy left Hollywood and returned to New York, where she rejoined the editorial staff of *New Masses*. Her experience in movieland now qualified her for the additional job of film reviewer.

Joy's movie column in *New Masses* became a controversial asset to the paper as she took her revenge on Hollywood. She made acid remarks about the decadence and hypocrisy of the Hollywood product and was merciless in her criticisms. For example she described the final scenes of *Tobacco Road* as being "dragged out like the deathbed scene in *East Lynne*"; and she condemned the Hedy Lamarr and James Stewart comedy, *Come Live With Me*, for having laughs that were "spaced as widely as a seven-year-old's teeth." She nevertheless confessed to liking any movie with the Marx Brothers—since they were all Marxists!

In 1940 *Anya* was published to universal acclaim. Wrote the *Saturday Review of Literature,*

> It is the full-blown beautifully written work of a deep artistic intelligence.... Miss Davidman has a natural flair for fresh and immediate seeing, and a sure knowledge of the swells and starts of emotion. Better, she can write what she sees and knows.

Determined to do everything she could for the further-ance of communism, Joy became a member of the League of American Writers, an organization founded ten years earlier to fight, among other things, "Imperialist war and fascism ... white chauvinism ... persecution of minority groups ..." and "the influence of bourgeois ideas in American liberal-ism," as well as to defend "the Soviet Union against capitalist aggression."

There was certainly no shortage of causes for which the communist could fight: the war in Spain had come to an inglorious end in 1939 with the fascists victorious, but now another, more dramatic battle was being waged against fas-cism in Europe. Believing passionately in the power of verse, Joy compiled a volume of anti-imperialistic war poetry for the League of American Writers.

War Poems of the United Nations contained 300 poems by 150 poets, including Carl Sandburg, Boris Pasternak, and Joy's mentor, Stephen Vincent Benét. There were also a good many unknown contributors and at least two en-tirely fictional ones—Hayden Weir and Megan Coombes-Dawson—created by Joy for the undercontributed English section.

Among the poems included was one entitled "Last Kilome-ter" by William Lindsay Gresham. He was not a particularly

97

talented poet, though he was later to achieve some success as a novelist. He was also to become Joy's husband.

Bill Gresham had been born in Baltimore in 1909. Since his mother came of strong Presbyterian stock, the young Bill was baptized, but religion played little part in his life thereafter. "My mother," he later wrote, "was vaguely agnostic, vaguely Fabian Socialist. What my father's religious beliefs were I never knew."

In 1917, the Greshams moved to New York City, where Bill graduated from high school in Brooklyn in 1926. Bill was a gifted youngster with a creative imagination, but there was in his character a restlessness and an uncertainty that he personally blamed on his background:

> My family were flotsam of the old South, drifting through an industrial world with no guide save legends of a golden age when their ancestors had been slaveholders and gentlefolk. . . . My parents had no coherent view of the world and so could give me none.

Bill's parents separated when he was in his teens, leaving him—even more unstable—to pursue a directionless career. A short-lived ambition to be a Unitarian minister made way for a variety of jobs: singing folk songs in the cellar clubs of Greenwich Village; enlisting in the Civilian Conservation Corps; working his way up from an office boy on the New York *Evening Post* to become a music, movie, and book reviewer; and then quitting journalism for a job as a copywriter in a small advertising agency.

Bill married a wealthy New Yorker, but the marriage quickly foundered because of his undisciplined drifting. When, in 1937, his best friend was killed at the Battle of Brunete in Spain, Bill rushed to volunteer for the Abraham Lincoln Brigade, which was engaged in helping the fight against Franco's fascist army. He was, by this time, a Marxist and a member of the Communist party of the United States. He was later to recall,

I spent fifteen months in Spain and never fired a shot. In the collapse of the Republic, the Internationals were hurried over the border to safety. I came home to the bitterness of a lost war, a light attack of tuberculosis, and a long nightmare of neurotic conflict within me.

In the wake of the fascist defeat of communism, Bill grew contemptuous of the high-sounding rhetoric of the party meetings. Once so inspiring, this now seemed to resemble "a phonograph record with the needle stuck: endless debates on who was going to bell the cat."

Worse than this disillusionment was Bill's personal dissatisfaction with his life. His marriage finally came to an end:

I was alone, and I had neither strength nor courage enough even to get out of bed. My will was paralyzed; the prospect of action of any sort filled me with panic. I realized that I was mentally ill. . . .

Bill consulted a social-worker friend who referred him to a psychoanalyst, but his condition worsened. He eventually decided that life wasn't worth living:

I hanged myself with a leather belt, to a hook in a closet. . . . Whether it was an accident or the intervention of a Power greater than myself, I shall never know in this life. At any rate, I came to myself on the floor—the hook had pulled out of the wall. . . . The suicidal impulse had met reality at last; life won!

Realizing just how ill he now was, Bill visited a psychiatrist and submitted to a course of Freudian psychoanalysis:

Through the next years runs a visible theme of mental healing, emotional growth, and the building of a more normal life. And, as a counter-point, a theme of spiritual seeking. . . .

99

This seeking took various forms—yoga, meditation, and (via the work of the Russian mystic P. D. Ouspensky) tarot cards.

Bill went through an extremely difficult period: tuberculosis had left him physically weak; analysis was revealing deep-seated anger against his parents, himself, and the ideologies he had embraced; his spiritual questing was, in reality, little more than aimless wandering from island to island in the archipelago of mysticism. At the same time, he was witty, intelligent, and exceptionally charming. This was the complex character with whom Joy Davidman fell in love.

They were married by a justice of the peace in Peterborough, New Hampshire, on Sunday, August 2, 1942. "If Joy had searched systematically for the wrong mate," observed her biographer, Lyle Dorsett, "she could not have improved on William Lindsay Gresham." It is easy to see, however, why Joy became so infatuated with Bill. He was a good-looking man—six feet tall, slim of build, dark eyed, and deep voiced, with a strong animal magnetism. Joy, on the other hand, was not particularly attractive—acquaintances at the time remember her as dumpy and unfeminine—so to have won the attentions of such a handsome man was no mean achievement.

There were other qualities in Bill to which Joy undoubtedly responded—a certain wildness she probably wanted to tame and a vulnerability that made her protective toward him. There was much, too, which they had in common—a passion for writing, an allegiance to communism, and a strong social awareness.

What neither of them could have acknowledged was that they were drawn to each other for deeply selfish reasons: to Bill, Joy offered the hope of finding a purpose for his existence, an anchor for his drifting life; to Joy, Bill represented the opportunity of physical fulfillment and an escape route from her parents.

Bill and Joy moved into a small apartment on East 22nd Street, and their problems began almost immediately. To begin with, there was a chronic shortage of money. Bill was writing, but finding it difficult to sell much more than the occasional short story, and Joy's work for *New Masses* brought in only $25 a week (a large proportion of which went to Bill's continuing psychoanalysis).

Then Bill began to drink heavily. For some time, he had resorted to alcohol when problems and worries got too much for him or when he found the revelations of his psychoanalyst too disturbing. Now, however, the drinking bouts became more frequent and more sustained.

Bill was researching a novel about carnival people and began to make regular visits to a bar at the Dixie Hotel, where many of them used to congregate. Eventually, the drinking became more important than the research. Bill was spending money that could be ill afforded and, as a result of his drinking, found it increasingly difficult to write.

Joy decided that something had to be done and she engineered a move to a new home in Sunnyside, Queens, which was conveniently distanced from Bill's habitual drinking venues. Money, however, was still in short supply, and the best they could afford was another small, cramped apartment in an area which Bill described as a "human filing cabinet."

The difficulties which Joy and Bill faced served only to deepen their dissatisfaction with communism. Bill wrote,

As a philosophy to live by, Marxist materialism is a fair-weather friend. While a man is busy and can sink his identity in a feeling of "mass-solidarity," it may give his life an illusion of meaning. It can carry him through hunger and even police beatings. But let a crisis occur in his own mind, and Marxism will fail him. It offers the individual no personal moral guidance. Its ethical principle—the only "good" is what best serves the interests of the working class—hides at its core a contempt for the individual and his needs unless his hardships can be dramatized for propaganda.

101

For Joy, a new dimension was to enter her thinking when she became pregnant:

> One of the Soviet novels popular at the time had a heroine who let a Nazi commander shoot her newborn baby rather than betray her comrades. I was just having a baby. In any such dilemma I knew I would do otherwise, and let the comrades take care of themselves. Perhaps it was reality coming in to displace imagined reality.

On March 27, 1944, her first child, David, was born. She later recalled,

> So far as ethics were concerned, I realized that if the interests of my baby ever collided with the interests of the Party, the Party could go hang. This worried me a little, but there is nothing like having kids to make you discover what you are instead of what you think you are. . . .

The following year, Joy contributed her last review to *New Masses* and resigned her associate editorship; on November 10, 1945, a second child, Douglas, was born.

For Bill, however, the births of his sons created fresh problems. He was completing work on his carnival novel, *Nightmare Alley*, and the interruptions of two small babies distracted him from writing and drove him to renewed bouts of drinking. He also began what was to be the first of several extramarital affairs. Joy was deeply hurt, but concealed her pain for the sake of the children.

Coping with this accumulation of problems, and trying to raise a family in cramped surroundings, left Joy with little time to write. She contributed a few antiwar poems to a volume entitled *Seven Poets in Search of an Answer*, but her chief concerns were surviving the day-to-day dramas of existence rather than seeking any ideological solution to life:

> By 1946, I had two babies; I had no time for Party activity, and I was glad of it; I hardly mentioned the Party except with

impatience. And yet, out of sheer habit, I went on believing that Marxism was true. Habit and nothing more. For I had no knowledge of divine help, and all the world had lost faith in gradual progress. . . .

It was during this period of mounting disillusionment that Joy discovered the books of C. S. Lewis. Her love of fantasy literature made it perfectly natural and easy for her to read the works of a writer who sprang from that very tradition—Lewis had even introduced George MacDonald as a character in *The Great Divorce.*

Another of his books that was to prove a major influence on her life was *The Screwtape Letters.* The demonic correspondence captured her imagination while challenging some of her most preciously held philosophies:

> Your man [Screwtape tells his nephew Wormwood] has been accustomed, ever since he was a boy, to have a dozen incompatible philosophies dancing about together inside his head. He doesn't think of doctrines as primarily "true" or "false," but as "academic" or "practical," "outworn" or "contemporary," "conventional" or "ruthless." Jargon, not argument, is your best ally in keeping him from the Church. Don't waste time trying to make him think that materialism is *true!* Make him think it is strong, or stark, or courageous—that it is the philosophy of the future. That's the sort of thing he cares about. . . .

Joy began to think seriously about a great many things—including God. In the meantime, however, in the hope of dealing with her immediate problems—Bill's alcoholism and continuing infidelity—Joy persuaded Bill that they should move out of the city. In 1945, shortly after the birth of Douglas, the Greshams left New York for Ossining, twenty miles away in Westchester County, a district favored by literary folk whose political leanings were toward the left.

It was a new start, but although they had left some of their problems behind them, others were too major to be resolved merely by moving. Money was even more at a premium now that Joy was no longer writing, and Bill's drinking remained as heavy as ever, often leading to outbursts of violence during which he would assault Joy or the children—once smashing a bottle over Douglas's head.

"I found I could not stop drinking," Bill wrote a few years later. "I had become physically an alcoholic. And against alcoholism in this stage, Freud is powerless. . . ." Bill's alcoholism was only one outward sign of a far more serious illness: neurotic and insecure, stripped by analysts of anything he had ever believed in, he was now verging on the brink of total mental breakdown.

A crisis was inevitable. When it happened, it proved—at least for Joy—to be as much as anything else a crisis of faith. One of the Christian poets Joy had read (for the beauty of his verse, not his beliefs) was Francis Thompson. In his poem "The Hound of Heaven," Thompson depicted God as a great hound relentlessly pursuing him through life. Joy wrote,

> God was more like a cat. He had been stalking me for a very long time, waiting for his moment, he crept nearer so silently that I never knew he was there. Then, all at once, he sprang.

He sprang on a day in 1946, when Bill was in New York and Joy was at home in Westchester with the children. The telephone rang. It was Bill. He told Joy that he was having a nervous breakdown: "He felt his mind going, he couldn't stay where he was and he couldn't bring himself to come home. . . . Then he rang off." As Joy remembered it,

> There followed a day of frantic and vain telephoning. By night-fall there was nothing left to do but wait and see if he turned up, alive or dead. I put the babies to sleep and waited. For the first time in my life I felt helpless; for the first time my pride was forced to admit that I was not, after all, "master of my fate" and "the captain of my soul." All my defences—the walls of arrogance and cocksureness and self-love behind which I had hid from God—went down momentarily. And God came in.

Joy was conscious of someone in the room with her: "a Person so real that all my previous life was by comparison mere shadow play. And I myself was more alive than I had ever been; it was like waking from sleep."

Her perception of God lasted but a few seconds. "When it was over I found myself on my knees, praying. I think I must have been the world's most astonished atheist."

When people later explained away her experiences as being the invention of a desperate mind, Joy replied:

> My awareness of God was no comforting illusion, conjured up to reassure me about my husband's safety. I was just as worried afterwards as before. No; it was terror and ecstasy, repentance and rebirth.

Eventually, Bill came home: "He accepted my experience without question; he was himself on the way to something of the kind. Together, in spite of illness and anxiety, we set about remaking our minds."

Joy and Bill seriously began to search for a religious answer to the questions they had so long been asking. Joy turned, instinctively, to Judaism, but decided that she should investigate all religions:

> Some of them had wisdom up to a point, some of them had good ethical intentions, some of them had flashes of spiritual insight; but only one of them had complete understanding of the grace and repentance and charity that had come to me from God. And the Redeemer who had made himself known, whose personality I would have recognized among ten thousand—He was Jesus.

With Bill, Joy began rereading authors whose beliefs they had previously shunned or dismissed, and in particular the writings of C. S. Lewis. Wrote Bill,

> His books exposed the shallowness of our atheist prejudices; his vision illuminated the Mystery which lay behind the ap-

pearances of daily life. We used his books as constant reference points, and ... Lewis' clear and vivid statement of Christian principles served as a standard by which to measure the other religions we studied. Christianity outshone them as the sun outshines smokey torches.

As they pursued their search for truth, the last remaining vestiges of their Marxist philosophy disintegrated. Joy was to write that her "communism shrivelled up and blew away like withered tumbleweed; I cannot tell exactly when it went, but I looked and found it gone."

In 1946, the Greshams' fortunes took a turn for the better with the publication of Bill's novel, *Nightmare Alley*. A macabre tale (using the tarot card symbols as a running motif), it told the story of an alcoholic who bites off the heads of live chickens in a carnival sideshow to get the money for his drinking.

The publisher's advance did little more than meet some of the many debts that they had accrued, but shortly after publication Twentieth Century Fox bought the movie rights. Bill received the sum of $60,000, and it seemed as if life might now become a little easier. The film *Nightmare Alley* was released the following year, with Tyrone Power and Joan Blondell in the cast. It was, said one critic, "a striking oddity."

The income from the film enabled the Greshams to move to a larger house—to an old mansion, in fact, complete with a colonnade, shuttered windows, and twenty-two acres of land—in romantically named Pleasant Plains.

Life seemed more settled there, and Joy reveled in the pleasures of rural life: growing her own vegetables and harvesting the wild strawberries and mushrooms that grew on the grounds. She also returned to writing, with a second novel, *Weeping Bay*, set in a small fishing community on Quebec's Gaspé Peninsula.

The book is filled with vivid characters such as the old man who operates the generators for a carnival that comes to the town and who is also a Protestant lay preacher. When one of the fishermen expresses his mistrust of priests, he replied, "Maybe Jesus don't need no priest for His telephone wire. Maybe the blessed Carpenter has got Him a way of boring a hole right straight into a man's heart. Ever figure on that, brother?"

Nevertheless, the local priests play an important part in the story of *Weeping Bay*, and in particular the former fisherboy M. L'Abbe Francois-Xavier Desrosiers who, at the end of the novel, receives (and repudiates) a vision of Jesus:

> . . . The voice spoke again, as clear in his mind as the voice of his own thoughts, and yet Other.
>
> "No man can serve two masters," it said, "for either he will hate one, and love the other; or else he will hold to the one, and despise the other. Choose, therefore."
>
> "Have I not chosen?" Desrosiers' thoughts said desperately. "Once for all, and long ago?"
>
> "No. Choose now."
>
> After a moment Desrosiers opened his eyes and stood up . . . he felt himself seized by a wild joy, an impulse to do he knew not what, mad things—to fling his biretta into the St. Lawrence and caper upon the mountaintops like a young goat. His whole life appeared to him, minute and clear, a life of small decencies, small vanities, small fears. For a long moment he hung poised between that gray and dusty life and the terrible joy.
>
> In that moment, Desrosiers denied his vision. He said the words which he had been taught. He said aloud, clearly, "These experiences as the Church tells us, are often sent to us as temptations of the Devil."
>
> He felt the pulse of his joy falter and tremble away into nothing. . . .

Bill was also writing a second novel, *Limbo Tower*, based on the experiences he had had in a tuberculosis sanitarium when he returned from Spain. He had now mastered his alcoholism: "By the spring of 1948," he wrote, "my drinking had begun to frighten me. Then something happened which is, I think, more important to the Christian than his own search for God. God sought me."

Realizing that nothing, not even the security of home, family, and money, took away the need to drink, Bill became panicky.

> A chemical change had taken place inside me. Drinking was no longer fun; it was a bitter necessity. And my personality was being poisoned by it. I had always been a genial, expansive drunk; now I was getting pugnacious and irrational. In despair my pride burst, and God could reach through to me. I admitted that I was powerless over alcohol; I admitted my defects of personality; I asked God to remove my faults and to help me to stop drinking. And my prayer was answered. Up until now I have never taken another drink. . . .

Bill wrote this in 1950 in one of a series of articles for *Presbyterian Life*. By then, he considered himself to be a Christian.

Joy had finally accepted the fact that she was an apostate and, she said, "The rest was fairly simple. I could not doubt the divinity of Jesus, and, step by step, orthodox Christian theology followed logically from it." In the summer of 1948, Joy and the two boys were baptized in the Pleasant Plains Presbyterian Church. Bill, baptized in childhood, became a member of the church by a confession of his faith.

The following year, Joy told the story of her life to Oliver Pilat of the *New York Post*. It was serialized under the title "Girl Communist: An Intimate Story of Eight Years in the Party." Concluding her denouncement of Marxism, Joy said: "It is not a case of bad men perverting a good philosophy . . . but a case of corrupt philosophy perverting many persons who start as unusually good and unselfish persons."

In 1951, Joy wrote "The Longest Way Round," an account of her conversion experience. It was published, along with the stories of twelve other converts to Protestant Christianity, in *These Found the Way*. Joy ended her contribution by speaking of her hopes for the future:

I want to go deeper into the mystical knowledge of God, and I want that knowledge to govern my daily life. I had a good deal of pride and anger to overcome, and at times my progress is heartbreakingly slow—yet I think that I am going somewhere, by God's grace, according to plan.

The same volume contained "From Communist to Christian" by William Lindsay Gresham, a reprint of his articles for *Presbyterian Life*. Describing his admittance into church membership, Bill wrote:

Baptized an Episcopalian, raised an agnostic, in turns a Unitarian, a hedonist, a stoic, a Communist, a self-made mystic, and an eclectic grabber after truth, I had at last come home.

But by the time *These Found the Way* was in the bookstalls, Bill was far less certain about what he believed. The "eclectic grabber after truth" was off in search of new perceptions, toying with Dianetics, Zen Buddhism, and the I Ching, as well as reviving his old interests in yoga and tarot. Bill's conversion had been short-lived—inspired, perhaps, more by Joy's experiences than by his own.

For a while, at least, he remained true to his resolution never to take another drink. "If I ever do," he had written, "it will mean that I have let anger or fear blot out God in my mind." His resolution to stay faithful to Joy, however, was soon abandoned.

Bill made no secret of his affairs, which he justified as being necessary in order to "recharge his batteries." But Joy, who was no longer prepared to tolerate his indiscretions, moved out of his bedroom. It was an acknowledgment that their marriage was virtually over.

A committed Christian, Joy was disappointed and depressed by Bill's behavior. She had hoped that they were embarking on a new life together, but things were again as bad as ever.

Joy had, however, one powerful source of spiritual encouragement. In 1950, through an introduction from the American writer Chad Walsh, she had begun a correspondence with the man whose work had played such an important part in her conversion: C. S. Lewis....

6

Surprised by Joy

An essential prerequisite for a happy life, C. S. Lewis once observed, was that a man "would have almost no mail and never dread the postman's knock." If true, then Lewis could have been seldom happy, for as his reputation grew, so too did his daily correspondence.

Some people wrote to thank him for his books or, occasionally, to take issue with them; others, responding to the highly personal style of Lewis's writing, confided their most intimate concerns to him and sought his advice.

Whatever their reason for writing, the majority of his correspondents had one thing in common: "It isn't chiefly *men* I am kept in touch with by my huge mail: it is *women*. The female, happy or unhappy, agreeing or disagreeing, is by nature a much more *epistolary* animal than the male."

Perhaps a more likely reason was that, for many women, Lewis's charisma as a guru was immeasurably heightened by his also being a highly eligible bachelor.

There were times when this was to cause Jack considerable embarrassment. In the early fifties he was repeatedly pestered by a woman who used to tell people that she and Lewis were engaged to be married. It finally reached a point where he ceased opening her letters. Undaunted, she placed an announcement of their wedding in the papers. Eventually, she arrived on his doorstep and had to be taken away.

If, as some have said, Jack was wary of women and shy in their company, it was doubtless an attitude prompted by experiences such as this.

The cranks aside, Jack dutifully answered all his correspondence even though to do so cost him dearly in terms of his creative time. Although the majority of the letters he received were little more than passing "fan mail," he did maintain a lifelong correspondence with some of those who wrote to him, as can be seen from his *Letters to an American Lady*, which was published posthumously.

Receiving as many letters as he did, it took some very particular quality for one of them to stand out from the rest. Just such a letter arrived on January 10, 1950. Warnie Lewis later wrote in his diary,

> She appeared as just another American fan, Mrs. W. L. Gresham from the neighbourhood of New York. With, however, the difference that she stood out from the ruck by her amusing and well-written letters.

Since these letters have not survived, there is no way of knowing what Joy wrote about or why her first letter so impressed Jack and his brother. No doubt she would have said something about the extent to which Jack's books—in particular *Miracles*, *The Great Divorce*, and *The Screwtape Letters*—had influenced her thinking. "Without his works," she wrote elsewhere about her conversion, "I wonder if I and many others might not still be infants 'crying in the night.'"

"Just another American fan" she might have been but Joy had hesitated for some while before writing, thinking perhaps that it was presumptuous to do so, and only did so in the end on the encouragement of Chad Walsh. She must have been particularly thrilled, therefore, when she received a letter in reply that was clearly more than a mere courtesy. She wrote to Chad Walsh,

> Just got a letter from Lewis in the mail. I think I told you I'd raised an argument or two on some points? Lord, he knocked my props out from under me unerringly. . . . I haven't a scrap of my case left. And, what's more, I've seldom enjoyed anything more. Being disposed of so neatly by a master of debate, all fair and square—it seems to be one of the great pleasures of life, though I'd never have suspected it in my arrogant youth. I suppose it's *unfair* tricks of arguments that leave wounds. But after the sort of thing that Lewis does, what I feel is a craftsman's joy at the sight of a superior performance.

This curious tone—self-effacing, yet at pains to identify herself with Lewis as a fellow craftsman—is an indication of just how complex Joy's feelings were toward Jack from the outset. For Jack, however, it probably meant little more than an excuse to indulge in some cerebral sparring of the kind he was used to having with his Oxford men friends. Whatever their reasons, Jack and Joy were soon enjoying a regular correspondence as "pen friends."

Conceivably there might never have been anything more to their relationship, if it hadn't been for one thing—Joy's unhappy marriage. It is hardly surprising that a woman in Joy's position should have derived so much satisfaction from corresponding with a man—romantically distanced from her by the Atlantic—who had played such an important role in her recent spiritual development, and with whom she had so many interests and beliefs in common. Every letter she received from Jack must have helped intensify

113

her dissatisfaction with life as Mrs. Gresham. She began to long for release.

Coincidentally, her pen friend in Oxford was suddenly released from a rather different tyranny. On January 12, 1951, at the age of seventy-nine, Mrs. Moore died of influenza. "And so ends," wrote Warnie in his diary, "the mysterious self-imposed slavery in which Jack has lived for at least thirty years."

Although Jack had devotedly provided and cared for his surrogate mother, Warnie found it hard to forgive Mrs. Moore for the way in which her ceaseless, thoughtless demands had served as a permanent interruption to everything that his brother had worked at, from studying for his First to the writing of *The Screwtape Letters*.

Warnie later said that he couldn't remember Jack working for more than half an hour without interruption:

> Down would go the pen, and he would be away perhaps five minutes, perhaps half an hour: possibly to do nothing more important than stand by the kitchen range as scullery maid. Then another spell of work, then the same thing all over again. . . .

Was it, perhaps unconsciously, of his relationship with Mrs. Moore that Jack had written in one of Screwtape's early letters to Wormwood?

> It is, no doubt, impossible to prevent his praying for his mother, but we have means of rendering the prayers innocuous. Make sure that they are always very "spiritual," that he is always concerned with the state of her soul and never with her rheumatism. . . .
>
> [By doing this] his attention will be kept on what he regards as her sins, by which, with a little guidance from you, he can be induced to mean any of her actions which are inconvenient or irritating to himself.

However stoically Jack Lewis may have borne such irritations and inconveniences, they were now at an end. "Well," wrote Warnie, "God rest her soul, the chapter is closed." A new—and surprising—chapter was about to open.

In February 1951, a month after Mrs. Moore's death, Jack had the disappointment of being defeated by C. Day-Lewis for the Chair of Poetry at Oxford (by 194 votes to 173), but by June he was enjoying a new sense of freedom—and feeling somewhat guilty about doing so. He wrote to a friend,

> I specially need your prayers because I am (like the pilgrim in Bunyan) travelling across "a plain called Ease." Everything without, and many things within, are marvellously well at present.

The Lion, the Witch and the Wardrobe, which had been published in 1950, was followed by a sequel, *Prince Caspian,* and Jack was already at work on a third story about Narnia, *The Voyage of the "Dawn Treader."* At the time, Jack was rather disappointed at the sales of his first children's book:

> A number of the mothers, and still more schoolmistresses, have decided that it is likely to frighten children, so it is not selling very well. But the real children like it, and I am astonished how some *very* young ones seem to understand it.

In addition to the children's books, Jack was writing an account of *English Literature in the Sixteenth Century, Excluding Drama* for the *Oxford History of English Literature* (nicknamed, because it was so demanding, "the O Hell"). He was also at work at a piece of autobiography that he decided to call *Surprised by Joy.* The title was to prove rather more prophetic than reflective.

In September 1952, Jack Lewis received an invitation from Joy Gresham to have lunch with her at the Eastgate Hotel opposite Magdalen College.

Joy had come to England for two reasons: "I was so much under Bill's influence," she was to recall later, "that I had to run away from him physically and consult one of the clearest thinkers of our time for help."

Under considerable pressure, it is not surprising that Joy finally decided to "run away." There was the pain of Bill's persistent infidelity, disappointment that he had so quickly drifted away from Christianity, and a great deal of anxiety over money, for although Bill was still not drinking, he was finding it increasingly difficult to work.

Nor was it in the least surprising that the person Joy should have run away to see was Jack Lewis. Whatever vestige of love remained in her relationship with Bill, it was now heavily overlaid by feelings of fear, anger, and contempt. Small wonder that the clever Mr. Lewis—so sound and self-assured, so incisive and amusing—should have become increasingly attractive to Joy.

It was to be an ironic coincidence that eventually provided Joy with a means of escape. Early in 1952, she had received a frantic telephone call from a cousin, Renée Pierce, who was running away from her violent drunkard of a husband. Joy and Bill agreed to give Renée and her two young children a home. It was a generous gesture, and no one could have foreseen the devastating consequences that would follow.

The cousins got on well together, and their relationship was mutually beneficial. Renée was safe from pursuit, since her husband knew nothing of Bill and Joy, and in return she helped run the home—doing many of the chores Joy found a tiresome interruption to her writing.

Renée's presence had another, important effect on Joy's life. The more time the cousins spent together (they shared a twin-bedded room since Joy had left Bill's bed), the more Joy began to notice the differences between them: whereas Renée took great pride in her appearance and was always stylishly dressed, Joy cared little about her figure or her clothes and even rather relished her local reputation as an eccentric.

Gradually Joy began to emulate Renée; she lost a good deal of excess weight and started to take an interest in how she dressed and how she wore her hair. The result was extraordinary. Joy recovered something of her youthful beauty and found new confidence and self-respect.

Sharing a house with Renée gave Joy a fresh awareness of her own femininity and sexuality, while sharing a correspondence with C. S. Lewis stimulated her intellect and creative imagination. Her problem was that as Joy blossomed anew, she became increasingly conscious of being shackled, by old affections and a sense of Christian duty, to a man who seemed incapable of change.

In the summer of 1952, Joy asked Renée if she would look after Bill and the boys while she visited England. Renée agreed and, in August, Joy sailed for Liverpool. She was thirty-seven years old. One of her intentions was to finish writing *Smoke on the Mountain*, a book on the Ten Commandments, much influenced by C. S. Lewis's style of apologetics.

Emotionally and spiritually, Joy's destination was to be Oxford, but on her arrival she traveled first to London to stay with another of her pen friends, Phyllis Williams.

Within the month, Joy was in Oxford and, accompanied (or perhaps chaperoned) by Phyllis, was lunching with the man she had so long wanted to meet.

No account exists of that first meeting between Jack and Joy, so one can only speculate on what impression each made on the other. Jack obviously enjoyed the encounter, for he repaid Joy's hospitality with an invitation for her and Phyllis to lunch with him and Warnie at Magdalen.

For some reason (possibly alarm at such an obvious acceleration of the friendship), Warnie found himself unable to join his brother; so Professor George Sayer, a friend and former pupil of Jack's, was asked to make up the foursome.

The second lunch date was apparently a huge success, with Jack clearly impressed by Joy's stimulating conversation, as well as amused by her clever displays of wit. Not that Joy ever toyed with language merely to create an effect. Says Chad Walsh,

With her, language was not a game, but a means of saying with the utmost clarity and power what she wanted to say. Someone hostile to her might say she spoke with a touch of arrogance. More gently, one might say that she seemed to be a person who spoke with authority.

"Her mind," Jack later wrote, "was lithe and quick and muscular as a leopard."

Passion, tenderness and pain were all equally unable to disarm it. It scented the first whiff of cant or slush; then sprang, and knocked you over before you knew what was happening. How many bubbles of mine she pricked! I soon learned not to talk rot to her unless I did it for the sheer pleasure . . . of being exposed and laughed at.

The qualities which Jack soon came to admire in Joy were, though he may not have realized it, identical to the qualities which Joy had admired in Jack since the very beginning of their relationship.

It wasn't long before another luncheon party was being arranged at Magdalen for Joy to meet Warnie and one or two Oxford friends. "I was some little time in making up my mind about her," Warnie was to recall four years later.

She proved to be a Jewess, or rather a Christian convert of Jewish race, medium height, good figure, horn rimmed specs, quite extraordinarily uninhibited. Our first meeting was at lunch in Magdalen, where she turned to me in the presence of three or four men, and asked in the most natural tone in the world, "Is there anywhere in this monastic establishment where a lady can relieve herself?"

Joy's alarming combination of good looks, sharp intellect, and brashness of manner must have come as something of a surprise—or, more accurately, a shock—to Jack's friends. Women had never had anything to do with their intellectual circle. Even those, like Tolkien, who had wives were careful to keep their college lives, and all that belonged to them, segregated from their home lives. Here was Lewis breaking the rules, upsetting the conventions, and inviting a woman—not just any woman, but a loud, Jewish, American woman—into their exclusively masculine world.

What had come as a surprise to Jack was that a woman could be anything at all like a man. This one enjoyed walking, drinking beer, telling jokes, and having intellectual arguments "with no holds barred." Years later, assessing what had made Joy so appealing to him, Jack described her as having been

> all that any man friend (and I have good ones) has ever been to me. Perhaps more. If we had never fallen in love we should have nonetheless been always together, and created a scandal. That's what I meant when I once praised her for her "masculine virtues." But she soon put a stop to that by asking how I'd like to be praised for my feminine ones. . . .

As the months passed, Warnie noted in his diary that "a rapid friendship" developed between Jack and Joy. So much so, she was invited to spend Christmas at the Kilns. The visit lasted a fortnight and—despite certain anxieties on Jack's part about the domestic arrangements—was a great success. "Quite an experience it was, Christmas with the Lewises!" Joy told Chad Walsh.

> An enormous turkey, and burgundy from the Magdalen cellars to go with it; I stole a wineglassful to put in the gravy, and they thought it was practically *lèse majesté*—till they tasted the gravy. . . .

Joy had the time of her life. Jack read the completed manuscript of *Smoke on the Mountain* (which Joy had dedicated to him), offered some useful advice, but "liked it quite well, thank heavens," and promised to write an introduction for the book; he showed her some of his poetry, which Joy thought very good, and allowed her to read the proofs of the OHEL volume which, she warmly declared, would "make people sizzle."

Accompanied by Warnie they took long walks, on one of which they got caught in savage rain; Joy blistered her feet, and "Jack and Warnie had to practically pull me the last stretch. But it was great fun!" They visited all the best pubs ("some day *I'm* going to open a pub in Oxford"), had an outing to a pantomime ("where we roared enthusiastically at the oldest jokes and joined in the choruses of the songs"), and saw all the traditional tourist attractions of Oxford.

Joy was captivated by the "Sweet City with its dreaming spires," its ancient colleges, and narrow lanes; the bustle of the High, the tranquillity of the Deer Park, the regulated beauty of the Botanical Gardens standing on the bank of the sleepy Cherwell. She told friends: "I've never felt at home anywhere as I do in Oxford. . . ."

For Christmas, Jack gave Joy a very special present—a copy of *Diary of an Old Soul* by George MacDonald. The book had been signed by MacDonald and dated April 27, 1885, and to this Jack added a further inscription: "Later: from C. S. Lewis to Joy Davidman, Christmas, 1952."

They had, wrote Warnie, "many merry days together," and all three of them were conscious of the extent to which their friendship had grown. In the case of Joy's feelings toward Jack, however, friendship developed into something much deeper. Whereas she had once been in love with the idea of being in love with C. S. Lewis, she was now in love with the man himself.

Jack seems to have been oblivious to what Joy was feeling. Perhaps he should have foreseen how his acts of kindness toward Joy were capable of being misinterpreted but then his experience of women was very limited and, anyway, Joy was a married lady. Even if Joy told Jack something of the difficulties that she and Bill had had, he certainly had no idea just how bad things were between them. That he discovered only as Joy's stay at the Kilns was coming to an end and the time was nearing for her return to America.

Joy had received a letter from Bill. It was a long, rambling letter, but there was no doubt about what it had to say.

> Renée and I are in love and have been so since about the middle of August. If it had not been for our love I could not have come through this summer with as little anguish as I have for things have been rough financially.

Although Joy and Bill had written several letters to each other during Joy's absence, this was the first intimation that Bill was not only having a new affair, but that it was with her own cousin, someone to whom she had given a home and friendship.

Whatever her feelings may have been toward Jack Lewis, Joy had already decided that she had to make another attempt to save her marriage. At the end of the chapter in *Smoke on the Mountain* on the commandment "Thou shalt not commit adultery," Joy had written:

> Let us forget about what we stand to *get* out of marriage and concentrate on what we must *give*. Let us put all our charity and patience and justice and fortitude into our matings, so that they must become true marriages and cannot lapse into adulteries.

Now she was faced by a letter from her own husband who wrote:

> I understand, I believe, what resolutions you have made about coming home and trying to make a go of our marriage. But I feel that all such decisions are sacrifices of human life on the altar of willpower. . . . When physical attraction is gone from a relationship between a man and a woman, all the comradeship in the world will not bring it back, and between you and me it is gone and has been gone for years.

121

In asking for a divorce, Bill expressed the hope that Joy would marry "some really swell guy," then, when he and Renée were married, both families could live near each other, and "the Gresham kids could have Mommy and Daddy on hand." Bill concluded this bizarre proposal with the following understatement: "Obviously there is the question of your cooperation in this ideal solution."

Joy at once turned to Jack for advice. How familiar the situation seemed. Had he not received a dozen letters which began "Dear Mr. Lewis, I was married at the age of 20 to a man I didn't love"? His counsel, however, was perhaps surprising: he advised her to divorce Bill.

In January 1953, Joy sailed for America. "When she left," said Warnie, "it was with common regrets, and a sincere hope that we would meet again." They were indeed to meet again, very much sooner than any of them expected.

7

"The Lord Is My Shepherd, by Gum!"

A dultery," wrote Joy Davidman in *Smoke on the Mountain*, "occurs in many forms. . . . All, in practice, come to much the same thing: a corruption of the heart, a destruction of the home, an end to love. . . ."

Just months after she had written these words, Joy was experiencing the truth of them. She arrived home in New York in January 1953, and received a violent reception from Bill, who was drinking once more:

> Bill greeted me by knocking me about a bit. . . . Two days after he'd half choked me, he asked me in all seriousness, "Have you ever known me to do a brutal or unkind thing?"

The contrast between the happiness she had enjoyed in England and the misery waiting for her on her return could scarcely have been more dramatic. Finally realizing that she would have to relinquish all hope of saving her marriage, Joy agreed to Bill's request for a divorce, feeling that "it would be a blessing for me in the end. . . ."

For a while, however, the divorce proceedings had to wait, as there was not enough money to pay for a lawyer. Eventually, Bill filed for divorce in Miami on the grounds of desertion and incompatibility.

Meanwhile, Renée had left New York for Florida in order to file for a divorce from her husband. This she obtained and a year later, on August 5, 1954 (the day on which the Greshams' divorce became legal), she married Bill.

With the separation agreed upon, Joy began to make plans for a new life. She might have made a fresh start anywhere in America; she decided, however, to return to England, taking David and Douglas with her. "I've become a complete Anglomaniac," she wrote; "can't wait to transplant."

They traveled on the Cunard's *M. V. Britannia*, arriving at Liverpool in November 1953, and went from there, by train, to London, where Joy booked into the Avoca House Hotel in Belsize Park.

Here Joy encountered the first of what were to be a succession of problems. Bill had undertaken to send Joy $60 a week to help support the children and had promised that his first check would be waiting for her in London. It wasn't, and it was another five weeks before it arrived.

During this time, Joy was hard pressed to make ends meet and was having great difficulty in locating permanent lodgings where children were allowed. Eventually the proprietor of the hotel offered Joy a furnished flat in an annex across the street. It had two large rooms, a grand piano, and a garden. Linen and cleaning services were provided, but the bathroom and toilet had to be shared, and meals were served in the main hotel. It was, nevertheless, a home; in a letter to Bill, Joy wrote, "The Lord really *is* my shepherd, by gum!"

David and Douglas had mixed feelings about their new lives. David took a dislike to England from the beginning, while Douglas treated the situation as something of an adventure which could as easily be enjoyed as endured. Both boys, however, missed their father, Renée's children, and Renée herself, to whom they had grown quite attached during their mother's earlier visit to England.

The difficulties which David and Douglas experienced on being uprooted and taken to a foreign country were made worse by Joy insisting that they should be sent to a private boarding school. After visiting several, Joy chose Dane Court preparatory school at Pyrford, in Surrey, largely on the recommendation of Jack's friend, Roger Lancelyn Green, whose sons were already pupils there.

The fees were expensive and neither David nor Douglas was happy there, but Joy saw this as an opportunity to give the boys a good start in life. "As to what their careers will be," she wrote to Bill, "that's up to them: I only want them to have the kind of character and background that will fit them for what they choose."

In early December, Joy took the boys to Oxford for a four-day visit to the Kilns. "Last week," wrote Jack to one of his many correspondents, "we entertained a lady from New York with her boys."

> Can you imagine two crusted old bachelors in such a situation? It however went swimmingly, though it was very, very exhausting; the energy of the American small boy is astonishing. This pair thought nothing of a four mile hike across broken country as an incident in a day of ceaseless activity, and when we took them up Magdalen tower, they said as soon as they got back to the ground, "Let's do it again!"

Giving Bill an account of the visit, Joy reported that "both boys were a big success with the Lewises." Joy also described the hikes by which Jack had allegedly been so exhausted:

> Jack reverted completely to schoolboy tactics and went charging ahead with the boys through all the thorniest, muddiest,

125

steepest places; Warnie and I meanwhile trailing behind and feeling very old.

David was introduced to chess, "learning instantly and doing very well," while Douglas endeared himself by "sawing huge armfuls of firewood" for the open fires which the boys, and their mother, thought much superior to the central heating systems of America. Jack wrote,

> Without being in the least priggish, they struck us as being amazingly adult by our standards and one could talk to them as one would to "grown-ups"—though the next moment they would be wrestling like puppies on the sitting-room floor.

For Douglas, who was eight years old at the time (he had celebrated his birthday in the middle of a gale on the North Atlantic), meeting Jack was a memorable experience, if (at first) a little less dramatic than he had expected. He recalled later,

> My first impression was one of disappointment because when you're eight years old and you read books about princes fighting dragons, you rather expect the man who wrote them to wear armour—at least—and carry a sword, and Jack didn't. He was rather stooped, and balding with a lined, humorous, face; he looked like a benevolent and kindly old man, but it didn't fit with the image of a man who wrote great heroic sagas. But the disappointment only lasted about five minutes. . . .

In the hallway at the Kilns, Douglas noticed the huge dark oak wardrobe which stood there. Hardly daring to believe it might be true, the boy asked Jack if it was "THE Wardrobe." With a twinkle in his eye, the old man replied, "It *might* be!" Faith in enchantment was restored. "And it was years," says Douglas, "before I dared to hang a coat in that wardrobe!"

A new Narnian adventure, *The Silver Chair*, had recently been published, and Jack had just finished writing the fifth book in the series. This was *The Horse and His Boy*, and the young visitors were allowed to read it in typescript. When it was published in 1954, Jack dedicated the book "To David and Douglas Gresham."

For Joy there were the delights of long conversations to which she had as much to contribute as Jack. Both possessed areas of interest in which they were superior (in experience if not intellect) to the other: Jack's detailed knowledge of language, literature, and Christian doctrine was matched by Joy's knowledge of contemporary poetry and political thought. These were among the many topics of their conversations, with Joy additionally undertaking to enlighten Jack on the comparative cultures of Britain and America.

The visit came to an end and the friends parted, all of them (with the exception of Warnie) facing a new phase in their lives.

Joy was faced with the realities of living, and raising a family, alone. When she left America, she had told her friend Chad Walsh that one reason for going to England was that "living is so much cheaper there and I'll be able to live decently on what Bill can pay." She was, however, anxious about her financial situation, adding, "Knowing him, I'm very doubtful whether he will pay for long." Her prognostication had from the outset proved uncomfortably accurate.

It wasn't long before Joy was facing real financial difficulties, not just with meeting the rent on her apartment (twelve guineas a week), but with finding the school fees for the boys' education.

David and Douglas had begun studying at Dane Court in January 1955. Jack must have had a particular understanding of how the new boys felt, for, after nearly thirty years at Oxford, he was beginning a new career as professor of medieval and Renaissance literature at Magdalene College, Cambridge.

Shortly before leaving Oxford, he wrote to a friend:

I think I shall like Magdalene better than Magdalen. It's a tiny college (a perfect cameo architecturally) and they're all so

127

old-fashioned, and pious, and gentle and conservative—unlike this leftist, atheist, cynical, hard-boiled huge Magdalen. Perhaps from being the fogey and "old woman" here I shall become the *enfant terrible* there. It is nice to be still under the care of St. Mary Magdalene: she must by now understand my constitution better than a stranger would, don't you think?

However, he may well have written in this vein in the hopes of convincing himself, as much as anyone else, that he didn't mind the prospect of change. Joy received what was probably a truer impression of his feelings. "Poor lamb!" she wrote.

He was suffering all the pangs and qualms of a new boy going to a formidable school—he went around muttering "Oh, what a fool I am! I had a good home and left!" and turning his mouth down at the corners most pathetical. He always makes his distress into a joke, but of course there's a genuine grief in leaving a place like Magdalen after 30 years; rather like a divorce, I imagine. . . . The Cambridge college is nothing like as beautiful, though pleasant enough; and Lewis has just written to say they only get *one* glass of port after dinner, instead of Magdalen's *three*!

Jack visited Joy in London on several occasions but, while his new post at Cambridge meant (as he put it) "rather less work for rather more money," it was time consuming having to commute each week to what Oxonians refer to as "the other place."

Joy found her new life of freedom increasingly difficult to cope with. Financial hardship kept her working at her typewriter for sometimes ten or twelve hours at a time, and this left her little opportunity to make friends and alleviate the loneliness she felt.

Joy's personality and background did not make it particularly easy for her to strike up acquaintances in England. Fortunately, she was befriended by a few of Jack's friends—in particular, June and Roger Lancelyn Green and the Reverend Dr. Austin Farrer and his wife, Katherine.

The English publication of *Smoke on the Mountain* occurred in 1955. Few of its readers could have guessed how intensely personal parts of it were:

> ...There *are* marriages which *God* puts asunder—cases of desertion and presumed death, cases of danger to body and soul, cases where children must be saved at all costs from a destructive parent.

Jack had written the foreword to the book in which (apart from pointing out that Joy's American language was "not always lexically or idiomatically the same as ours") he commented on the author's particular suitability to write on the subject of the Commandments:

> In a sense, the converted Jew is the only normal human being in the world. To him, in the first instance, the promises were made, and he has availed himself of them. He calls Abraham his father by hereditary right as well as by divine courtesy. He has taken the whole syllabus in order, as it was set; eaten the dinner according to the menu. Everyone else is, from one point of view, a special case, dealt with under emergency regulations. . . .

Helped by the association of C. S. Lewis's name, *Smoke on the Mountain* did quite well in England, selling three thousand copies (against half that number in the United States), but royalties took time to accumulate and Joy remained desperately short of money.

The Lewises did what they could, and she typed manuscripts for Jack and compiled an index for one of Warnie's several books on seventeenth-century French history. Soon, however, Jack was having to help with gifts of money and, when Bill stopped sending cash, he took on the responsibility of paying the boys' school fees.

Some people have suggested that Joy pressured Jack into giving her financial help, but everything in his character suggests that he responded to her needs out of simple Christian charity. Writing to one of his correspondents, who was also in the position of having to accept financial assistance from friends, Jack wrote:

> We are all members of one another and must all learn to receive as well as to give. . . . Isn't the spiritual value of having to accept money just this, that it makes palpable the total dependence in which we always live anyway?

In the summer of 1955, Jack accepted even greater responsibility for Joy's problems by suggesting that she should move to Oxford. He found a suitable house for her that was only a mile away from the Kilns and insisted on paying the rent. In August, Joy and the two boys moved into 10 Old High Street, Headington.

"She and Jack began to see each other every day," Warnie recalled some years later, adding that "it was now obvious what was going to happen."

Visiting Joy in Oxford, Chad Walsh "smelt marriage in the air," but one can only speculate on the nature of Jack and Joy's relationship at this time.

It is unlikely that Jack was, in any sense that he would have understood, "in love" with Joy, although she was undoubtedly very much in love with him and, in the opinion of some, determined to marry Jack, come what may.

By now, of course, marriage was no longer an impossibility—by the time Joy moved to Oxford, she and Bill were legally divorced and he was remarried—except, of course, that both Jack and Joy had very strong ideas about the position of the Christian in such circumstances. As Joy had written in *Smoke on the Mountain*: "Our Lord's command about marriage was as sharp and straight as a sword. Your wife is your wife for good, he said; you can't get rid of her, except for adultery (and only one Gospel permits even that exception) and a divorced woman is committing adultery if she remarries."

Whatever they may have written or believed, Jack and Joy clearly gave people the impression that their relationship was growing into something rather more than mere affection. Joy made a few friendships in Oxford (she became especially close to Katherine Farrer), but since her friends were also Jack's friends, they were inevitably seen together and thought of by others as a couple.

Certainly by the time Jack's autobiography, *Surprised by Joy*, was published there was a good deal of Oxford gossip about him and Joy. Although Jack appears to have been oblivious to the double meaning of the title, there were plenty of people who were not, and the popular joke in Oxford at the time was that C. S. Lewis really *had* been "surprised by Joy."

As the friendship between Jack and Joy grew, he began to ask her opinion on the things he was writing and to take notice of her criticisms. Although Joy knew that she could not write "one-tenth as well as Jack," she felt perfectly able to "tell him how to write more like himself." Joy had read and discussed Jack's autobiography with him and was doing the same with the new book he was working on. Jack told her with great kindness (and probably, by this stage, truthfulness) that he found her advice indispensable. The book was a retelling of the legend of Cupid and Psyche that he called *Bareface*, but which was eventually published as *Till We Have Faces* because the publishers thought the proposed title made it sound too much like a western!

For many people, *Till We Have Faces* is C. S. Lewis's finest book (although it is stylistically unlike anything else he ever wrote); and the central character of Psyche's sister, Orual, is clearly inspired by, if not modeled on, that of Joy Davidman. Wrote Roger Lancelyn Green and Walter Hooper,

> Orual's spiritual journey parallels Joy's pilgrimage from her Jewish background by way of atheism and communism, until her conversion to Christianity. There is also in a sense the physical Joy, the middle-aged and not particularly good-looking

woman whom Lewis was able to treat for a long time almost as one of his men friends. . . .

One of the male characters in the novel has just such a relationship with Orual: they begin by sharing a deep (but sexless) affection for one another; gradually, however, Orual falls in love with the man even though he remains unable to reciprocate her passion for him.

It was a situation that Jack was to consider in greater depth in his book *The Four Loves*, where he wrote:

> In most societies at most periods Friendships will be between men and men or between women and women. The sexes will have met one another in Affection and in Eros but . . . they will seldom have had with each other the companionship in common activities which is the matrix of Friendship. . . . But in a profession (like my own) where men and women work side by side, or in the mission field, or among authors and artists, such Friendship is common.

He then goes on to look at a potential difficulty that may arise from close friendships between members of the opposite sex:

> What is offered as Friendship on one side may be mistaken for Eros on the other with painful and embarrassing results. Or what begins as Friendship in both may become also Eros. . . .

At different times in his relationship with Joy, both situations were true for C. S. Lewis.

Joy, however, still had her problems. When in October 1955, Bill wrote to say he had secured a permanent job, Joy replied that she was delighted "for your sake as well as my own." Bill's payments to her had become very few and far between. So although Joy's letter continued with a relaxed account of the family—"Doug is on the under-eleven football team and they've won a match; Davy is corresponding with Professor Tolkien about runes; Warnie has been reading and enjoying *Monster Midway*" (Bill's latest book about carnivals) "though the carny world rather horrifies him"—she eventually returned to the thorny subject of money.

Joy made it perfectly clear that while she appreciated Bill's financial difficulties, she needed "dough immediately," adding, "I will *not* go to Jack with my hand outstretched. Once was enough. So come across, please!"

Bill responded with a small payment. "Well, every bit helps." She wrote in acknowledgment, "Mercy drops falling around me etc; but O for the showers I need: I notice you don't say how much you are being paid: I conclude it is at least $100 a week and probably more. I appreciate the fact that you've other obligations, but please don't put us last on your list."

To bring home her point, Joy told Bill that she could not afford to buy any coal for the fire: "Never mind, I've just bought a quid's worth of old roadblocks—the tar-impregnated wood blocks from the London streets. They burn beautiful. . . ."

Despite the financial constraints under which she lived, there were plenty of happy times:

> We had a terrific Guy Fawkes weekend—fireworks are cheap here; the boys shot them all off themselves and were very careful, no casualties except to some marigolds which are still blooming in the garden.

Joy was even becoming established as something of an Oxford celebrity. In 1955 she was invited to lecture students at Pusey House on the subject of Jack's old friend Charles Williams. She observed,

> It's funny enough that I should be lecturing to Oxford students; but still funnier that I should be talking about Williams here, where he lived for years and so many people knew him. What a world!

133

Then, in 1956, Joy faced a new crisis. The British Home Office refused to renew her visitor's visa, which meant that she and the boys would have to uproot themselves once more and return to America.

There was only one way in which Joy's expulsion could be avoided and that was if she could somehow acquire British citizenship. The obvious way in which she could do that was to marry a British subject. It is not known how Jack found out about this solution—whether he made legal inquiries himself, or whether Joy informed him. Whichever was the case, Jack decided to marry Joy.

Jack may have been anticipating the likelihood of such an event for some months, for in the autumn of 1955, he wrote enigmatically to his old friend Arthur Greeves,

> . . . The other affair remains where it did. I don't feel the point about a "false position." Everyone whom it concerned would be told. The "reality" would be, from my point of view, adultery and therefore mustn't happen. (An easy resolution when one doesn't in the least want it!)

On April 23, 1956, Jack and Joy were married at the Registry Office in Oxford. The witnesses were Austin and Katherine Farrer.

Two days later, Jack told Roger Lancelyn Green about the marriage, saying that it was "a pure matter of friendship and expediency" and that his solicitor had drawn up a legal document stating the reasons for the marriage having taken place.

Writing later, in his diary, about the secret wedding, Warnie wryly observed: "The gap between the end of the *Ancien Régime* and the Restoration had lasted for less than four years." He added that Jack had assured him

> that Joy would continue to occupy her own house as "Mrs. Gresham," and that the marriage was a pure formality designed

to give Joy the right to go on living in England: and I saw the uselessness of disabusing him.

This last remark suggests that, at least in Warnie's mind, matters were not quite as simple as Jack made them appear; he continued:

> Joy, whose intentions were obvious from the outset, soon began to press for her rights, pointing out with perfect truth that her reputation was suffering from Jack's being in her house every day, often stopping until eleven at night. . . .

Then a fresh problem arose. For some reason, Joy was given notice to quit her house. Although Jack didn't really regard the civil ceremony they had gone through as, in any sense, a Christian marriage (and despite the concern that his relationship with Joy should not become an adulterous one), he decided that Joy and her sons would have to live with him. "All arrangements had been made," wrote Warnie, "for the installation of the family at The Kilns, when disaster overtook us. . . ."

Late on the evening of October 18, 1956, Katherine Farrer had a sudden premonition that something was wrong with Joy. She dashed to the telephone and began to dial her friend's number. Before it could ring, Joy—who was carrying a tray of tea things in from the kitchen—tripped over the telephone wire and fell. Joy felt the bone in her leg snap and a surge of excruciating pain. She was incapable of moving, but beside her on the floor was the telephone receiver and at the other end the anxious voice of Katherine Farrer.

Joy was rushed to the Wingfield-Morris Orthopaedic Hospital and her broken leg was examined. For some while Joy had been in pain with what she presumed to be rheumatism. As the months had passed, the pain had worsened. But it was not, she now discovered, rheumatism. It was cancer.

The disease had eaten through her left femur and so weakened the bone that, when she fell, it had snapped like a dry stick. There was also a malignant lump in her breast.

For Jack it marked the return of a grisly specter from the past. Listening to the doctor's doomful diagnosis, all the anguish and terror of his mother's illness and death must have come flooding back to him.

"No one," Jack once observed, "can mark the exact moment at which friendship becomes love." This, however, was as good a moment as any; as he tried to take in the fact that he might soon be parted from Joy, so he began to realize just how agonizing that parting would be for him.

Jack insisted that the seriousness of Joy's condition should not be kept from her: "I would allow no lies to be told to a grown-up and a Christian. As you may imagine," he wrote to a friend,

> new beauty and new tragedy have entered my life. You would be surprised (or perhaps you would not?) to know how much of a strange sort of happiness and even gaiety there is between us.

Now, when Joy was physically at her least attractive, she won Jack's heart. Jack wrote,

> Years ago, when I wrote about medieval love-poetry and described its strange, half make-believe, "religion of love," I was blind enough to treat this as an almost purely literary phenomenon. I know better now. . . .

Jack's love for Joy—and the pain which was part of it—deepened with every passing day. He wrote to his old friend Arthur Greeves: "It will be a great tragedy for me to lose her," and to another friend: "I can hardly describe to you the state of mind I live in at present—except that all emotion, with me, is periodically drowned in sheer tiredness, deep lakes of stupor. . . ."

Shortly before the storm had broken, Jack had published *The Last Battle*, the seventh and final Chronicle of Narnia; in it the characters come, at last, to a paradise garden:

> ... They found themselves facing great golden gates. And for a moment none of them was bold enough to try if the gates would open.... "Dare we? Is it right? Can it be meant for *us*?"
>
> But while they were standing thus, a great horn, wonderfully loud and sweet, blew from somewhere inside that walled garden and the gates swung open....

8

A Deeper Magic

A marriage has taken place between Professor C. S. Lewis, of Magdalene College, Cambridge, and Mrs. Joy Gresham, now a patient in the Churchill Hospital, Oxford. It is requested that no letters be sent.

This announcement appeared in the personal column of the *Times* on Christmas Eve, 1956.

Joy had been moved to the Churchill Hospital earlier in December after having three major operations. Jack began to prepare for whatever might follow. David and Douglas were moved into the Kilns, and Jack decided that he wanted to publicly confirm the private formality of his marriage to Joy.

It was probably around this time (although Warnie recalls it as happening earlier) that the Bishop of Oxford was approached and asked to grant the necessary permission for Jack and Joy to receive a Christian marriage.

In November, while Joy was still undergoing operations, Jack told the American lady with whom he regularly corresponded: "I may soon be, in rapid succession, a bride-groom and a widower. There may, in fact, be a deathbed marriage."

But the Bishop of Oxford refused to sanction the marriage. It had been argued that since Bill had entered into a secular marriage before he met Joy, and since Bill and Joy's marriage had happened before either of them became Christians, that when Joy had met Jack she was not really married in any Christian sense. Discussing this argument, Father Walter Hooper has said: "If marriage (even a secular one) is *indissoluable* then Gresham was still married to his first wife: if only Christian marriage is indissoluble, William Gresham and Joy Davidman were never married."

In any event, the official position of the Church of England was, as it still is, that remarriage by a divorced person is, according to Scripture, an act of adultery. It is, therefore, impossible for the Church to approve of such a union, let alone bless it with the sacrament of marriage.

However insensitive—even intolerant—such a ruling may seem, the Bishop of Oxford had no choice but to refuse. To make an exception in the case of so eminent a Christian as C. S. Lewis was obviously unthinkable.

Jack was left with no alternative but to make public the fact that he was, anyway, legally married to Joy. In a letter to Arthur Greeves, Jack explained,

> If she gets over this bout, and emerges from hospital, she will no longer be fit to live alone so she must come and live here. That means (in order to avoid scandal) that our marriage must shortly be published.

A few weeks later, Jack placed his carefully worded announcement in the *Times*.

Concluding his letter to Arthur, Jack wrote: "I know you will pray for her and for me: and for Warnie, to whom also, the loss if we lose her, will be great."

Warnie had, some time before, overcome his reservations about Joy and now felt a strong brotherly affection for her. "I have never loved her more," he wrote in his diary,

> than since she was struck down; her pluck and cheerfulness are beyond praise, and she talks of her disease and its fluctuations as if she was describing the experiences of a friend of hers. God grant that she may recover. . . .

But Joy did not recover. By the following March, when she was once again in the Wingfield Hospital undergoing radiation treatment, her condition had so far deteriorated that Warnie recorded in his diary: "One of the most painful days of my life. Sentence of death has been passed on Joy, and the end is only a matter of time."

Joy now had feelings of terrible despair: "I am in rather a bad state of mind as yet," she wrote to friends.

> They had promised me definitely that the x-rays would work; I'd pinned all my hopes to having a year or so of happiness with Jack at least—and indeed it seems I shall lie about in the hospital with my broken femur waiting for death, and unable to do anything to make my last shreds of life useful or bearable. . . . I am trying very hard to hold on to my faith, but I find it difficult; there seems such a gratuitous and merciless cruelty in this. . . . I hope all we have believed is true. I dare not now hope for anything in *this* world.

Encouraged and supported by Jack, Joy rallied a little; enough, in fact, to write again to her friends:

> I feel now that I can bear, not too unhappily, whatever is to come, and the problem of pain just doesn't loom so large—I'm not at all sure I didn't deserve it after all, and I'm pretty sure that in some way I need it. . . . Jack pointed out to me that we were wrong in trying to accept utter hopelessness; uncertainty is what God has given us for a cross.

141

Although Joy described everything as looking "much brighter than it did before," her condition was still worsening. Since there was nothing that the doctors could now do for Joy, and since Jack was determined that she should not have to face death in a hospital, he asked for permission to take her home. The request was granted.

There remained, however, the question of whether or not they were married in the sight of God. It has been suggested (by Warnie among others) that the civil marriage ceremony had meant far more to Jack at the time than a mere act of charity. But if this had been the case, then the couple would have seen no obstacle to their now living together as man and wife. As it was, they both considered it essential that their union be blessed by God.

A solution to the problem came quite unexpectedly, when Jack invited a friend and former student, Peter Bide, to visit the Kilns. As a priest, Peter Bide had several times had experiences that led him to believe that he possessed the gift of Christian healing. He had confided these experiences to Jack and discussed with him the concept of faith healing.

Jack had an open mind on the subject. He considered praying for the sick to be "unquestionably right," but was cautious about prayers accompanied by anointing or laying on of hands: "Whether any individual Christian who attempts Faith Healing," he once wrote,

> is prompted by genuine faith and charity or by spiritual pride is I take it a question we cannot decide. That is between God and him. Whether the cure occurs in any given case is clearly a question for the doctors. . . .

What led him to the opinion that Peter Bide possessed a God-given gift was that the young man was extremely reticent about claiming to have performed miracles and had such a strong sense of his own unworthiness that he could not possibly have been accused of spiritual pride. Jack asked him to lay hands on Joy and pray for her recovery.

When Peter Bide agreed, Jack raised the question of the marriage. He had no right, of course, to ask Father Bide to perform a service the bishop himself had refused to conduct, but Jack was desperate to make what looked like Joy's final days as bearable as possible.

Writing many years later to Joy's biographer, Father Bide explained: "It did not seem to me in the circumstances, possible to refuse her the outward and visible sign of grace which she so ardently desired and which might lead to a peaceful end to a fairly desperate situation." The decision to marry Jack and Joy according to the service of the Church of England prayer book was, as Warnie described it, "a notable act of charity," if for no other reason than because Peter Bide must have known that the action would earn the severe displeasure not only of his own bishop, but of a bishop to whose diocese he did not even belong.

The marriage took place in the stark, sanitized setting of the Wingfield Hospital at eleven o'clock in the morning of Thursday, March 21, 1957. The bride lay propped up on pillows and the bridegroom sat on the side of the bed while the sad little ceremony was conducted by Father Bide and watched by Warnie and one of the nursing sisters who attended Joy.

There was a terrible poignancy about the exchange of vows, as Jack and Joy promised to be faithful to each other "for better for worse, for richer for poorer, in sickness and in health, to love and to cherish, till death us do part."

"I found it heartrending," wrote Warnie, "especially Joy's eagerness for the pitiable consolation of dying under the same roof as Jack; though to feel pity for anyone so magnificently brave as Joy is almost an insult." After the marriage, Father Bide laid his hands on Joy and prayed for her recovery.

Jack knew just how hopeless Joy's condition was, but he would not have been human if he hadn't entertained a hope, however feeble, that she might be healed. Did he perhaps recall the words he'd written ten years before in *Miracles*?

> We must not picture destiny as a film unrolling for the most part on its own, but in which our prayers are sometimes allowed to insert additional items. On the contrary; what the film displays to us as it unrolls already contains the results of our prayers and of all our other acts. There is no question *whether* an event has happened because of your prayer. When the event you prayed for occurs your prayer has always contributed to it. When the opposite event occurs your prayer has never been ignored; it has been considered and refused, for your ultimate good and the good of the whole universe.

A week after the marriage, Joy was taken home to the Kilns by ambulance and installed in the sitting room. "Every moment," wrote Jack, "is spent at her bedside," despite the fact that a resident hospital nurse was in attendance. A month later, Jack was writing to a friend that he was leading "the life of a hospital orderly, and have hardly time to say my prayer or eat my meals."

There were also David and Douglas to be looked after ("gruelling work for two old bachelors!"), but however ill-equipped he and Warnie were for the task of bringing up two young boys, they did have one very particular qualification in that the youngsters were "facing the very same calamity" that had befallen them as boys. Douglas remembers Jack taking him and his brother to visit their mother in the hospital and explaining to them that she had cancer: "He did it well—far better than his father had managed so many years before...."

Adding to Jack's problems was the fact that Warnie—who for some years had had a drinking problem—was often incapable of giving his brother the help he needed. Nevertheless, Warnie was acutely aware of the painfulness of Jack's situation: "There seems little left to hope," he wrote in his diary, but that there may be no pain at the end. How glibly one talks of "resignation," and how difficult it is to practice; *why*, one asks, should Jack have had the life which has been his—the best 32 years of it eaten out by [Mrs. Moore], and then the prospect of "peace at eventide" so cruelly snatched away.

Concluding this melancholy entry, Warnie wrote: "How rapid the whole thing has been," and recalling, perhaps, that January day in 1950 when the first letter arrived from Mrs. Joy Gresham, he added: "Seven years ago we didn't even know that such a person as Joy existed."

As if things weren't difficult enough for Jack, Bill decided to write to Joy that in the event of her death, he wanted David and Douglas to return to America. It was Jack who summoned up the determination and strength of character to reply:

> . . . Your letter reached Joy after a day of agony. The effect was devastating. She felt that the only earthly hope she now has had been taken away. You have tortured one who was already on the rack; heaped extra weights on one who is being pressed to death. There is nothing she dreads so much as a return of the boys to your charge. You perhaps do not understand that certain scenes (when you were not yourself) came early enough in their lives to make you a figure of terror to them. Their return to the USA when their education is finished is, of course, quite a different matter. Now, bitterly against their will, coming on top of the most appalling tragedy that can happen to childhood (I went through it and know), tearing them from all that has already become familiar, and shattering all sense of security that remains to them, it would be disastrous. If you realized the cruelty of what you are proposing to do, I am sure you would not do it.

In response to Bill's demand that the boys should return to him if Joy died, Jack replied:

145

What you and I have to think of is the happiness of the boys. . . . There is no question of your resigning yourself to "never seeing them again." Why should there not be a real, unconfused, reconciliation between you and them when they are growing up? But by forcing them back at a moment when their hearts are breaking, you will not facilitate this but render it permanently impossible. The boys remember you as a man who fired rifles throu' ceilings to relieve his temper, broke up chairs, wept in public, and broke a bottle over Doug's head. David knew, and resented, the fact that you were living with your present wife while still married to his mother. Children have indelible memories of such things and they are (like us adults) self-righteous. . . .

Leaving Bill in no doubt that if the matter were pursued, "every legal obstacle" would be placed in the way of the boys' return, Jack ended:

You have a chance to soothe, instead of aggravating the miseries of a woman you once loved. You have a chance of recovering at some future date, instead of alienating forever, the love and respect of your children. For God's sake take it and yield to the deep wishes of everyone concerned except yourself.

It was enough to make Bill relent.

A few weeks after Joy's homecoming, Jack was writing to Roger Lancelyn Green: "Joy is completely bedridden . . . but, thank God, no pain, sleeping well, and often in good spirits." Jack, however, *was* in pain. He had prayed that God would let him bear some of Joy's discomfort for her. Not long afterward, Joy began to find relief while Jack developed excruciating pains in his legs. The doctors diagnosed Jack to be suffering from calcium deficiency: "No one suggests that the disease is *either* curable or *fatal*. It normally accompanies that fatal disease we call senility, but no one knows why I have got it so early in life," at the same time Joy—who needed calcium badly—was found to be making more.

146

But Jack remained cautious about Joy's slight improvement in condition—remembering no doubt his mother's apparent recovery. "Though the doctors hold out no ultimate hope," he wrote in May,

> the progress of the disease does seem to be temporarily arrested to a degree they never expected. There is little pain, often none, her strength increases and she eats and sleeps well. This has the paradoxical result of giving her lower spirits and less peace. The more *general* health, of course, the stronger the instinctive will to live. Forbidden and torturing hopes will intrude on us both. In short, a dungeon is never harder to bear than when the door is open and the sunshine and birdsong float in. . . .

As the months passed, their hopes continued to build: "Joy is to all appearances (blessedly or heartbreakingly) well and anyone but a doctor would feel sure she was recovering. . . ."

Soon, however, the doctors themselves were wondering whether Joy's condition might not be improving. The cancer, it seemed, had been arrested: the diseased spots in the bone were no longer multiplying. Then, as Jack put it, "the tide began to turn." The cancerous spots began to disappear and new bone was being made.

By September, Joy was up and sitting in an invalid chair. Two months later she wrote, in a letter to Bill, that she could "now climb two or three stairs, walk fifty feet or so, sit nearly normally, and use the John like the big folks—and no small triumph that!" She was given a raised shoe and by December was walking about the house and garden: "limping," wrote Jack, "and with a stick, but *walking.*" This was real, undoubted progress and Jack was forced to accept that, however unlikely, Joy was recovering.

> She even found herself getting up *unconsciously* to answer the telephone the other day. It is the unconsciousness that is the real triumph—the body that would not obey the most planned volition now begins to act on its own. . . . *Of course*, the sword of

Damocles still hangs over us; or should I say, we are forced to be aware of the sword which really hangs over all mortals?

By March 1958, Joy's condition was still improving. Roger Lancelyn Green dined at the Kilns and recorded in his diary that Joy was "up and about, miraculous as it seems." In July, Joy accompanied Jack to see Douglas's prize giving at Dane Court. The miracle, it seemed, had happened.

In a letter to friends, Joy wrote:

> My case is now arrested for the time being. I may be alright for three or four years. . . . Jack and I are managing to be surprisingly happy considering the circumstances: you'd think we were a honeymoon couple in our early twenties, rather than our middle-aged selves. . . .

They took a few days away together, about which Jack happily remarked: "I'm such a confirmed old bachelor that I couldn't help feeling I was being rather naughty ('staying with a woman at a hotel!' Just like people in the newspapers!)"

Just as their love for each other had been heightened by the threat of separation, so now it was given a new intensity by Joy's reprieve. "Do you know," Jack told friends, "I am experiencing what I thought would never be mine. I never thought I would have in my sixties the happiness that passed me by in my twenties." Joy simply observed that "the movies and the poets are right: it does exist!"

"There were never two people alive in the history of the world," says Douglas Gresham, "who were more in love than Jack and Joy."

Joy's recovery, however much an answer to prayer, presented a problem for Warnie. When Joy had come to live at the Kilns, she had come there to die. There was no question of Warnie being de trop, but now things were rather different: Joy might well live for several years and, with her returning strength, was already beginning to express an interest in the running of the house—she told friends that she felt "Quite the lady of the manor!" It was time, perhaps, for Warnie to think about leaving. He wrote,

> For almost twenty years, I had lived under a matriarchy at The Kilns. Then had followed a few years of unfettered male liberty. And now The Kilns was once more to have a mistress. Upon one thing my mind was absolutely made up, and that was that never again for any consideration would I submit to the domestic condition which had prevailed under our *ancien régime*—and I sketched out provisional arrangements for an unobtrusive withdrawal from the home after the marriage, and the establishing of a home of my own in Eire.

Warnie's plans, however, were quickly forestalled:

> Before I could even hint at my intention, I discovered that it had never entered the heads of either Jack or Joy that I should do otherwise than continue to be one of the family at The Kilns; so obviously I had to give the new *régime* a trial before committing myself to my Irish plans.

This Warnie did, and found

> all my apprehensions permanently and swiftly dispelled. What Jack's marriage meant to me was that our home was enriched and enlivened by the presence of a witty, broad-minded, well-read, tolerant Christian whom I had rarely heard equalled as a conversationalist. And to crown all, one who had a deep interest in and a considerable knowledge of the seventeenth century, my own pet hobby. . . .

Indeed, Joy was soon advising Warnie on his new book, *The Scandalous Regent* (which he was to dedicate "To My Sister-in-law Joy Davidman"); and, more importantly, helping him to give up drinking—something for which the years of coping with Bill's alcoholism made her peculiarly suited.

Joy also gave Jack the benefit of her sharp mind: in conversation, to his great delight, she would often deflate his pomposity and cut him down to size. Douglas Gresham recalls one occasion when Jack was holding forth at great length at the dinner table and Joy cut in with a request that he "shut up and pass the pedanticide!"

To Jack's writing she brought a fresh, incisive critical approach that, on his own admission, helped him greatly with both *Reflections on the Psalms* and *The Four Loves*.

Reflections, Jack's first "religious" book in ten years, particularly benefited from the insights into Judaism which Joy gave him, and in a sense he could never have written *The Four Loves* if he had not fallen in love with, and married, Joy. Of *Reflections*, the *Church Times* said: "He has never written better. Nearly every page scintillates with observations which are illuminating, provocative and original." Certainly, Jack had never written with more maturity, tempering intellect with emotion, reason with experience:

> Our quarrels provide a very good example of the way in which the Christian and Jewish conceptions differ, while yet both should be kept in mind. As Christians we must of course repent of all this anger, malice and self-will which allowed the discussion to become, on our side, a quarrel at all. But there is also the question on a far lower level: Did we pretend to be angry about one thing when we knew, or could have known, that our anger had a different and much less presentable cause? Did we pretend to be "hurt" in our sensitive and tender feelings when envy, ungratified vanity, or thwarted self-will was our real trouble? Such tactics often succeed. The other parties give in. They give in not because they don't know what is really wrong with us but because they have long known it only too well, and that sleeping dog can be roused, that skeleton brought out of its cupboard, only at the cost of imperilling their whole relationship with us. . . . And so we win; by cheating. But the

unfairness is very deeply felt. Indeed what is commonly called "sensitiveness" is the most powerful engine of domestic tyranny, sometimes a lifelong tyranny.

There was, of course, nothing new about Joy showing an interest in Jack's work: she had done that from the time she had first come to live in England. Now, out of love (and gratitude) she extended that interest to the rest of Jack's life. She took over the management of his finances which—since he was hopeless at dealing with money—were utterly disorganized. Although he had no great fortune, Jack would often lose track of income from royalties, and be quite convinced that he was practically destitute while large forgotten sums (once as much as £900) were lying, unprofitably, in a current account at the bank.

Joy also began to improve the quality of life at the Kilns. For years the Lewises' bachelor premises had been so disreputable they had been referred to by Oxford friends as "the Midden" (a Middle-English word literally meaning "dung heap"): "Nothing has been done for thirty years," wrote Joy.

> The walls and floors are full of holes; the carpets are tattered rags—in fact, the house is being held up by the books that line the walls and if we ever move a bookcase All Fall Down!

But all did *not* fall down. Joy was soon having some "cautious painting and repair done." Holes in the roof were mended, and the central heating system, which had not been used since the war, began going again. Joy spent a little money on furnishings and curtains (always pretending that they had cost vast sums in order to outrage Jack, when they had invariably been purchased at sales), and generally made the Kilns not merely habitable, but homey.

Writing to Roger Lancelyn Green in May 1958, Joy told him:

The Kilns is now a real home, with paint on the walls, ceilings properly repaired, clean sheets on the beds—we can receive and put up several guests. . . . I've got a fence round the woods and all the trespassers chased away; I shoot a starting pistol at them and they run like anything! We'd love a visit.

Joy's renovations were also extended to Jack's wardrobe, which was purged of the torn jackets, battered hats, and elbowless pullovers which he was wont to wear. Although Jack occasionally feigned irritation and annoyance, he was secretly delighted by the transformation wrought by Joy. For the first time in years, he and Warnie were living in comfort.

Most of Jack's old friends accepted this new life-style of his because they could see the happiness and fulfillment it had brought him. However, some felt that in marrying Joy Gresham, Jack had betrayed their friendship and his own principles. Tolkien, particularly, found the whole thing "very strange." As a devout Catholic, he was deeply shocked to hear that his closest friend had entered into a marriage with a divorced person. He was also hurt at hearing the news from someone other than Jack himself, especially since he had taken Jack into his confidence about problems within his own marriage.

In July, Jack took Joy on a belated honeymoon to Wales and then to see the green hills and misty mountains of Ireland. They went by air (sea travel being thought too hazardous for Joy). "It was the first flight either of us had ever experienced," wrote Jack,

and we found it—after our initial moment of terror—enchanting. The cloudscape seen from above is a new world of beauty—and then the rifts in the clouds through which one sees "a glimpse of that dark world where I was born. . . ."

Joy adored Ireland. "We had a heavenly time," she told Bill in a letter, beautiful sunny weather, miraculous golden light over everything, clear air in which the mountains glowed like jewels . . . there's a good deal of austerity in its beauty, but it is the most beautiful place I've ever seen.

They visited Louth, Down, and Donegal and returned, wrote Jack, "drunk with blue mountains, yellow beaches, dark fuchsia, breaking waves, braying donkeys, peat-smell and the heather just beginning to bloom."

The days following Joy's recovery were filled with happiness—made all the sweeter for having been pried from the clutches of death. For both of them, life and love had been touched and transformed by a Deeper Magic from before the Dawn of Time.

9

Farewell to the Shadowlands

In January 1959, readers of *The Atlantic Monthly* would have come across an article by C. S. Lewis on "The Efficacy of Prayer":

> I have stood by the bedside of a woman whose thigh-bone was eaten through with cancer and who had thriving colonies of disease in many other bones as well. It took three people to move her in bed. The doctors predicted a few months of life: the nurses (who often know better), a few weeks. A good man laid his hands on her and prayed. A year later the patient was walking (uphill, too, through rough woodland) and the man who took the last x-ray photos was saying, "These bones are as solid as rock. It's miraculous."

And so, indeed, it seemed. By the autumn Joy was walking distances of up to a mile with relative ease. There were still a few small holes in her bones and the pain was invariably present. "It's not easy," she explained, "walking about with one thigh more than three inches shorter than the other." Yet she was "miraculously well and active." The hospital, she told Bill, "tell me I'm one of their great triumphs and exhibit me to visiting doctors. . . ."

In October 1959, almost two years after the cancer had begun to disappear, Joy went to the hospital for a routine X-ray. "This last check," wrote Jack, "is the only one we approached without dread. Her health seemed so complete. . . ." But, in fact, the X-rays showed that the cancer had returned.

In *Till We Have Faces*, Jack had made Orual ask:

> What do the gods expect of us? A prisoner may come to bear his dungeon with patience; but if he has almost escaped, tasted his first draught of the free air . . . to be retaken then, to go back to the clanking of that fetter, the smell of that straw?

He now used the same simile in writing of Joy's fate: "It is like being recaptured by the Giant when you have passed every gate and are almost out of sight of his castle."

The recovery, it appeared, was not really a recovery at all. It was, Jack wrote to his American lady friend,

> only a reprieve, not a pardon. There seems to be some hope of a few years' life still and there are still things the doctors can do. But they are in the nature of "rear-guard actions." We are in retreat.

Then, using a phrase he had used so differently only months before:

> The tide has turned. Of course, God can do again what he did before. The sky is not now so dark as when I married her in hospital. Her courage is wonderful and she gives me more support than I can give her.

Warnie had very similar feelings, remarking that Joy's courage and vitality were such "that one was able to forget the grim facts for hours and even days at a time." But the grim facts remained. The cancerous spots and lumps were in evidence again—so much so that Joy jokingly observed: "I've got so many cancers at work on me that I expect them to start organizing a union." And by March 1960, three years after the hospital wedding ceremony, those cancers were no longer responding to the radiation treatment.

Jack had once described his and Joy's existence as being lived under the sword of Damocles—the sword which, according to legend, was suspended by nothing more than a human hair. It was now only a matter of time before the hair snapped. Jack wrote,

> Meanwhile you have the waiting—waiting till the x-rays are developed and till the specialist has completed his observations. And while you wait, you still have to go on living—if only one could go underground, hibernate, sleep it out. And then the horrible by-products of anxiety; the incessant circular movement of the thoughts, even the Pagan temptation to keep watch for irrational omens. And one prays; but mainly such prayers as are themselves a form of anguish. . . .

That was how Jack recalled the agony of this period in retrospect, when writing his *Letters to Malcolm*. At the time, he tried to put his feelings into verse, in a poem entitled "Relapse" which ends:

> . . . all our former pain
> And all our surgeon's care
> Is lost, and all the unbearable (in vain
> Borne once) is still to bear.

Although the cancer was continuing to spread throughout her body, Joy fought hard against it. A combination of faith and willpower drove her on. She had also one burning ambition still to be fulfilled; to recapture the happiness of her honeymoon with Jack on another holiday. This holiday, however, would be somewhat further afield than the Emerald Isle—Joy wanted, more than anything, to visit Greece.

"Fair Greece!" wrote Byron, "sad relic of departed worth! Immortal, though no more; though fallen, great!" A fitting place, perhaps, for a final odyssey.

In 1959, the Lewises' friends June and Roger Lancelyn Green had toured Greece and, on their return, enthused so much that Jack said if they were to go again, he and Joy would like to go with them. Later that year, Roger booked the four of them onto a "Wings" tour for the following spring.

Although Jack had loved the tales of Ancient Greece since boyhood, he had never felt any desire to visit the land of their origin; to do so might detract from his imagined conception of the place. He had, in fact, shunned foreign travel altogether and had left the British Isles only twice in his life: once for a holiday near Dieppe when he was eight, and later during his war service in France. Now, however, Jack wanted to do everything he could to make what he felt sure were Joy's dying days as happy and memorable as he could.

Although careful not to communicate it, Jack must have felt considerable anxiety at the prospect of taking a very sick person on such a strenuous journey. Since he was himself suffering from osteoporosis and high blood pressure, he was hardly in any condition to cope if Joy were to be taken suddenly ill. It was of the greatest importance, therefore, that the holiday was going to be taken in company with understanding friends who would be willing and able to help if the need arose. Jack could scarcely have chosen two better traveling companions.

Roger Lancelyn Green had first visited Greece when he was an undergraduate at Merton College. He had fallen under the spell of the land and its literature and later wrote novels for children set in Ancient Greece as well as publishing his own masterly retelling of the great myths, *Tales of the Greek Heroes*. Roger's vivacious wife, June, a well-read and entertaining conversationalist, was an ideal companion for Joy.

With the return of the cancer, the holiday became less certain. Jack tried to remain hopeful, and in the same letter in which he had described to Roger Joy's recapture by the Giant, he wrote:

> Whether a second miracle will be vouchsafed us, or, if not, when the sentence will be inflicted, remains uncertain. It is quite possible she may be able to do the Greek trip next Spring. Pray for us.

By March 1960, Jack was clearly very worried. He told Arthur Greeves in a letter that

> cancer is returning in almost every part of her skeleton. They do something with radio-therapy, but as soon as they have silenced an ache in one place, one breaks out in another. The doctors hold out no hope of a cure.... We hope to do a lightning trip to Greece by air this vacation. We hardly dare to look as far ahead as next summer....

Although the odds were now heavily stacked against her, Joy struggled on. When spring came round, it found her all the more determined to make the visit. Cheerfully disregarding the doctors' warning that to go to Greece would be taking "a big chance," she wrote to Bill: "I'd rather go out with a bang than a whimper, particularly on the steps of the Parthenon!"

On Sunday, April 3, 1960, the Lewises and the Greens were seen off at London Airport by Douglas. In a small Viking plane they traveled via Lyon, Naples, and Brindisi to Athens.

Jack had deliberately not told Roger and June how desperately ill Joy had become, but they soon deduced, from the extent of her pain, that her condition was now incurable. At Athens, after what had been a rough flight, Joy had great difficulty in walking from the plane to the airport buildings. Recounting this in his diary, Roger added: "We immediately learnt the Greek for a wheelchair—which we shall demand in future."

159

The following day, Joy was not well enough to go with the party on a morning excursion to Marathon, and Jack stayed with her at the hotel. By midday, however, they were lunching with Roger and June, and joining the afternoon tour of Athens, "the eye of Greece, the mother of arts and eloquence."

Joy performed the first of several "prodigies" by climbing to the top of the Acropolis. There, on the steps of the Propylaea (the grand entrance to the citadel), Jack and Joy found a seat and, recalled Roger, "sat drinking in the beauty of the Parthenon and Erectheum—columns of honey gold and old ivory against the perfect blue sky, with an occasional white cloud."

On Tuesday, they visited Mycenae, the city of King Agamemnon and his son, Orestes, built (say the myths) by the one-eyed Cyclopes of Zeus. Jack was greatly impressed by the Lion Gate and the towering walls of huge stones, and he was deeply moved by being in the place where one of the great dramas of the ancient world had been enacted. "I shall never forget," wrote Roger, "the way he paused suddenly and exclaimed: 'My God! The Curse is still here,' in a voice hushed between awe and amazement."

Wednesday, April 6, was for both couples a red-letter day. Roger marked it down as "the most memorable day on the whole tour," adding that it was one "which Jack said afterwards was among the supreme days of his life—the last of the great days of perfect happiness." With a hired car and a driver who had only a smattering of English, they drove to Daphni. Here they visited the temple of Apollo and the famous Byzantine Church with its vast mosaic portrait of Christ filling the dome and dominating the entire building: symbols of the old religion and the new standing almost side by side.

"I had some ado," Jack later recalled,

to prevent Joy (and myself) from relapsing into Paganism in Attica! At Daphni it was hard not to pray to Apollo the Healer. But somehow one didn't feel it would have been very wrong—would have only been addressing Christ *sub specie Apollinis*....

From Daphni they drove to Eleutherae and explored the ancient fortress with its mighty walls eight feet thick, and then on through "richly scented pine woods" and "olive groves shining silver in the sunlight" to the tiny coastal village of Aegosthena, where, beside the shore of the Gulf of Corinth, they drank ouzo and retsina and dined on fried squid, red mullet, ewe's milk cheese, and freshly picked oranges.

Writing of this day in his diary, Roger Lancelyn Green said:

> We sat there for several hours, the usual vivid conversation lapsing into contented silence broken only by the gentle lapping of the waves, the pervading hum of bees and the call of cicadas: the misty blue of the Gulf and the miraculously clear light of Greece working a charm of absolute contentment....

In the days that followed, the Lewises and the Greens visited Herakleon (in Crete), Knossos, Rhodes, and many other historical sites. All of them enjoyed exploring the classical ruins and the small Grecian villages, sampling local wines and dishes. Meals were invariably accompanied by sparkling conversation. "Usual hilarious dinner with Jack and Joy," Roger noted one day, and on another: "Splendid verbal sparring between Jack and Joy, each enjoying it to the full: we could barely keep up with them...."

An amusing incident at one of these meals was recorded by Roger on April 10, when they were in Crete:

> We were kept waiting hours for a very indifferent meal, and the band blared away deafeningly. Joy finally began flicking bread-pellets at the nearest musician, and the four of us whiled away the time by writing alternate lines of the following doggerel:

Jack: A pub-crawl through the glittering isles of Greece,
Joy: I wish it left my ears a moment's peace!

161

June:	If once the crashing Cretans ceased to bore,
Roger:	The drums of England would resist no more.
Jack:	No more they *can* resist. For mine are broken!
Roger:	To this Curetes' shields were but a token,
June:	*Our* cries in silence still above the noise—
Joy:	He has been hit by a good shot of Joy's!
Jack:	What aim! What strength! What purpose and what poise!"

But for all the happiness and camaraderie, Joy was far from well. Toward the end of the holiday, she hurt herself getting up and down the high step to the coach, and from then on she and Jack would follow the coach party in a hired car. Whenever they stopped, Roger had a ritual task to carry out:

> We'd realized for some time that Joy was often in pain, and alcohol was the best alleviation: so I had become adept at diving into the nearest taverna, ordering "tessera ouzo," and having them ready at a convenient table by the time June had helped Jack and Joy out of the coach or car and brought them in.

Shortly before his death, Jack reflected on the time in Greece, telling Father Walter Hooper:

> Joy knew she was dying, I knew she was dying, and *she* knew *I* knew she was dying—but when we heard the shepherds playing their flutes in the hills, it seemed to make no difference.

Here in this earthly paradise garden, they stood upon the very frontier of Aslan's country; how effortless it seemed to contemplate saying farewell to the shadowlands. . . .

The holiday drew to an end, and the four friends flew home via Pisa, arriving in London on April 14. Concluding his diary of the holiday, Roger Lancelyn Green wrote: "My last sight of Joy was of Jack wheeling her briskly in an invalid chair towards the waiting car."

Despite the anxieties and some problems, the trip had been a great success. In a letter to his publisher, Jocelyn Gibb, Jack wrote: "Greece was wonderful. We badly need a word meaning 'the-exact-opposite-of-a-disappointment.' *Appointment* won't do!" Five days after their return, Jack wrote to his American lady correspondent saying how difficult he found it to describe Greece:

> Attica is hauntingly beautiful and Rhodes is an earthly paradise—all orange and lemon orchards and wild flowers and vines and olives, and the mountains of Asia on the horizon. . . .

Joy he described as being

> very exhausted and full of aches. But I would not have had her denied it. The condemned man is allowed his favourite breakfast even if it is indigestible. She was absolutely enraptured by what she saw. But pray for us: the sky grows very dark. . . .

Joy's condition now began to deteriorate quickly, making their time in Greece all the more precious to them. Writing to Chad Walsh, Jack said that Joy had come back "in a *nunc dimittis* frame of mind, having realized, beyond hope, her greatest, lifelong, this-worldly desire." There had been, however,

> a heavy price to pay in increased lameness and leg-pains: not that her exertions had or could have any effect on the course of cancer, but that the muscles etc, had been overtaxed. Since then there has been a recrudescence of the original growth in the right breast which started the whole trouble. It had to be removed last Friday—or, as she characteristically put it, she was "made an Amazon." This operation went through, thank God, with greater ease than we had dared to hope. . . .

Joy's mastectomy was carried out on May 20, just five weeks after she and Jack returned from Greece. Two weeks later she was home again and, as her jesting description of the operation

163

suggests, was in good spirits. Warnie described her as having "emerged from the ordeal radiant," and the surgeons spoke in encouraging terms of her condition.

Although confined once more to a wheelchair, Joy refused to sit back and wait to die. She kept up her correspondence, giving helpful advice to Bill, who was planning a visit to Oxford in the autumn, and got Warnie to push her to the library and out into the Kilns' garden so that she could inspect the flower beds and greenhouse.

Then, suddenly, Joy was taken ill once more. For several days she had been complaining of indigestion.

When it got worse and was accompanied by retching and vomiting, the doctor was called in and diagnosed her suffering as a gastric infection. During the night of Sunday, June 19, she became much worse and by the middle of the next morning told her nurse, "This is the end, I know now I'm dying. Telegraph for Doug."

The cancer, it seemed, was now in her gall bladder and liver. Joy was taken by ambulance to the Acland Hospital, where she told the doctor: "Finish me off quick, so I won't have another operation." But no operation was possible. She was given drugs and soon drifted into a coma. "There is nothing now left to pray for," said Warnie, "but that she may die without recovering consciousness."

Jack was at the hospital when the boys returned home. "I met David at the bottom of the drive," Warnie wrote in his diary,

> and broke the position to him as gently as I could. . . . Poor Doug arrived in tears, having heard the news from his headmaster . . . and has been very miserable ever since, though the resilience of his age protects him from the worst of the shock. Telephone ringing with kindly futile enquiries most of the afternoon. . . .

Then, in a telling postscript, Warnie added: "Forgot to say that dear Joy was still well enough and thoughtful enough to make me a present of a dozen handkerchiefs on my 65th birthday, last Thursday 16th."

The end, it seemed, had finally come. A week later however, Warnie was writing: "Once again Joy has made fools of the doctors and nurses." She had recovered and was home again, ". . . but all the time there is the grim knowledge that it cannot be more than a reprieve." Nevertheless, Douglas returned to school where, as head prefect, he had to take part in the end-of-term service.

A few days later, Joy and Jack had Sunday lunch at Studley Priory hotel. The following day she was taken for a car ride into the Cotswolds. For Jack and Warnie, anxiety was tempered with the kind of optimism that is so often born of desperation.

On the night of July 12, Warnie took tea in to Jack and Joy in the downstairs room that had become Joy's bedroom:

> I found her looking remarkably better, and she herself said she felt much more comfortable . . . when I left her she was playing scrabble with Jack; and before I dropped off to sleep they sounded as if they were reading a play together. . . .

Later Jack was to write: "How long, how tranquilly, how nourishingly, we talked together the last night!" Joy had once said to Jack, "Even if we both died at exactly the same moment, as we lie here side by side, it would be just as much a separation as the one you're so afraid of." Later, perhaps on this very night, Jack asked her: "If you can—if it is allowed—come to me when I too am on my death bed." "Allowed!" she replied, "Heaven would have a job to hold me; and as for hell, I'd break it into bits." "She knew," wrote Jack,

> she was speaking a kind of mythological language, with an element of comedy in it. There was a twinkle as well as a tear in her eye. But there was no myth and no joke about the will, deeper than any feeling, that flashed through her.

At 6:15 on the morning of Wednesday, July 13, Warnie was awakened by terrible screams. Downstairs, he found Joy writhing in agony. He roused Jack, and the doctor was called. Within an hour, drugs were being pumped into her but, due to her tremendous resistance, did little more than make her drowsy.

The next few hours were a frenzy of activity as Jack tried unsuccessfully to get Joy admitted to a hospital. Finally, he succeeded in persuading her surgeon to give her a bed in his private ward at the Radcliffe Infirmary. At 1:30, the ambulance arrived, and Jack traveled with Joy to the hospital.

What a rabble of memories must have crowded into Jack's mind during that journey. Was this really the man who, just a handful of years before, had remarked that he could not understand why anyone should choose to marry a *woman*, since every topic of conversation would be used up in the first six months? Strange then that but a few days ago he should have written with such passion and such anguish:

> All this flashy rhetoric about loving you.
> I never had a selfless thought since I was born.
> I am mercenary and self-seeking through and through:
> I want God, you, all friends, merely to serve my turn.
>
> Peace, re-assurance, pleasure, are the goals I seek,
> I cannot crawl one inch outside my proper skin:
> I talk of love—a scholar's parrot may talk Greek—
> But, self-imprisoned, always end where I begin.
>
> Only that now you have taught me (but how late) my lack.
> I see the chasm. And everything you are was making
> My heart into a bridge by which I might get back
> From exile, and grow a man. And now the bridge is
>   breaking. . . .

He called the poem, "As the Ruin Falls." It ends:

For this I bless you as the ruin falls. The pains
You give me are more precious than all other gains.

The afternoon and evening passed gently with Joy dozing.
When she was awake, however, she was fully aware of all that
was happening. She asked Jack to give her fur coat as a parting
gift to Katherine Farrer, and told him that she wanted Austin
Farrer to read her funeral service. She asked to be cremated,
adding, "Don't get me a posh coffin; posh coffins are all rot."

As the evening wore on, the surgeon called Jack from the
room. Joy, he told him, was now rapidly dying. When Jack
went back to her, he told her that the end was near; it was,
she replied, the best news they could now have.

Then Austin Farrer gave Joy final Absolution:

Almighty God, our heavenly Father, who of his great mercy
hath promised forgiveness of sins to all them that with hearty
repentance and true faith turn unto him: Have mercy upon
you; pardon and deliver you from all your sins; confirm and
strengthen you in all goodness; and bring you to everlasting
life; through Jesus Christ our Lord. . . .

Turning to Jack, Joy told him, "You have made me happy."
Then, a little while after, "I am at peace with God."

Joy died at 10:15 that evening.

"She smiled," Jack later recalled, "but not at me."

. . . As they went on they got the strangest impression that
here at last the sky did really come down and join the earth—a
blue wall, very bright, but real and solid: more like glass than
anything else. And soon they were quite sure of it. It was very
near now.

But between them and the foot of the sky there was something so white on the green grass that even with their eagles'
eyes they could hardly look at it. They came on and saw that
it was a Lamb.

"Come and have breakfast," said the Lamb in its sweet
milky voice.

167

Then they noticed for the first time that there was a fire lit on the grass and fish roasting on it. They sat down and ate the fish, hungry now for the first time for many days. And it was the most delicious food they had ever tasted.

"Please, Lamb," said Lucy, "Is this the way to Aslan's country?"

"Not for you," said the Lamb. "For you the door into Aslan's country is from your own world."

"What!" said Edmund. "Is there a way into Aslan's country from our world too?"

"There is a way into my country from all the worlds," said the Lamb; but as he spoke his snowy white flushed into tawny gold and his size changed and he was Aslan himself, towering above them and scattering light from his mane. . . .

10

A Grief Observed

I'd seen violent death," Jack later wrote, "but I'd never seen a natural death before. There's nothing to it, is there?"

He returned home from the hospital and broke the news to Warnie, who wrote in his diary, late that evening: "God rest her soul. I miss her to a degree which I would not have imagined possible."

Many years later, Warnie was to reflect upon his brother's life with Joy, describing it as

> a short episode, of glory and tragedy: for Jack, the total (though heartbreaking) fulfilment of a whole dimension to his nature that had previously been starved and thwarted.

But now, as in other moments of great crisis in his life, Warnie turned to drink. Many years ago, when another tragedy had struck their lives, Jack and Warnie had been like "two frightened urchins huddled for warmth in a bleak world." Now, Jack stood alone.

Once again, Douglas was recalled from school. This time it was too late; his mother was already dead. "I arrived back at The Kilns," he later recalled,

> walked in through the front door and into the common-room. Jack was standing by the fireplace. That man had aged twenty or thirty years in the week since I had seen him last.

Although convention told the fourteen-year-old boy that he should not display any emotion, he was unable to contain his grief. "I looked at him, and simply said: 'Oh, Jack!' and burst into tears." Then Jack did what was, for him, an extraordinary thing—he embraced Douglas.

A man with many male friends and companions, Jack could "never endure the embrace or kiss of my own sex." It was, he once wrote, a weakness in his character, adding: "an unmanly weakness by the way; Aeneas, Beowulf, Roland, Launcelot, Johnson, and Nelson knew nothing of it."

Parenthood might have enabled him to overcome this inhibition, but becoming a stepfather was scarcely enough to effect a cure. Nevertheless, he now crossed the room, and took Douglas in his arms. They clung to one another for a minute or more. "It was," says Douglas, "the first and only physical display of affection between us."

"Well," said Jack, as they broke apart, "I suppose we just have to get on with living. . . ."

Monday, July 18, 1960—the day of Joy's funeral—was, wrote Warnie, "a sunny, blustering day, with big white clouds." At 11:15, Jack, together with Warnie, David, and Douglas, left the Kilns in a taxi; following in a second car were the Lewises' housekeeper and her husband, and Joy's nurses. "At the roundabout," Warnie's account continues, by chance, not design—we fell in behind the hearse, and for the last time, poor dear Joy drove along the road to Studley. Except for the Farrers, none of Jack's friends bothered to put in an appearance at the service. . . .

Why were Jack's friends so conspicuously absent? Was it, as has been suggested (and as Jack believed), a demonstration of their true feelings about Joy and his marriage to her? Some may have resented Joy, even viewed her as a gold digger who had somehow wormed her way into Jack's life, but this does not explain why those who had already accepted Joy as a friend should not have been present.

Several of them, like Roger Lancelyn Green and his wife, simply did not know that Joy had died. Of those who did, Douglas Gresham believes, many would have found it "an intolerable burden to witness Jack's grief."

The funeral, as Warnie recalled it, was in "a nice, simple, sunlit chapel, with 'thank God' no music." The service itself was "poorly read by Austin (under great emotional strain)," something that affected Douglas deeply. "One of the hardest things I've ever had to do," he remembered, "was to listen to Austin Farrer trying to read that service through his tears and not cry myself."

It was a heartbreaking affair, and a pathetic exit for such a vibrant, courageous soul. "At the end," concluded Warnie,

the coffin was withdrawn and curtains, pulled invisibly, hid it from us for ever. There is no doubt that cremation is the most dignified ending; Joy really has become dust, returned to dust in clean sunlight. . . .

They left the chapel at Headington Crematorium and made their way back to the cars; past the trees and flower beds of the garden of remembrance. Years earlier Jack had written, in answer to a question from one of his correspondents, that he preferred trees to flowers in the sense that if I had to live in a world without one or the other, I'd choose to keep the trees. I certainly prefer tree-like people to flower-like people—the staunch and knotty and storm-enduring kind to the frilly and fragrant and easily withered.

In Joy he had met a woman who combined the best qualities of both types of person: staunch, yet fragrant, she had endured the storms while other friends had withered away.

Jack began to try to go on living. It was anything but easy. He had once glibly remarked, "There's nothing discreditable in dying: I've known the most respectable people do it!" But was it not, somehow, discreditable to grieve? "He didn't cope with his grief," says Douglas,

> he suffered his grief—he suffered enormously with it. Sometimes, someone would bring up a reference to Mrs. Lewis, and Jack would burst into floods of uncontrollable tears.

The heroine of *Till We Have Faces* says, of a different kind of loss: "It was as if my whole soul had been one tooth and now that tooth was drawn. I was a gap." So it was for Jack. He wrote to his American lady friend: "I can't describe the apparent unreality of my life. . . . I'm like a sleepwalker at the moment. . . ."

Yet, to whom could he turn for comfort, this man to whom others were constantly turning for help? Not his disciples, or colleagues, or friends. Not his brother, not the boys. "I cannot talk to the children about her," he wrote.

> The moment I try, there appears on their faces neither grief, nor love, nor fear, nor pity, but the most fatal of all non-conductors, embarrassment. They look as if I were committing an indecency. They are longing for me to stop. I felt just the same after my own mother's death when my father mentioned her. It's the way boys are. . . .

He was, says Douglas, "incapable of understanding that if he kept on talking about my mother, I was going to burst into tears—what embarrassed me was that fear. . . ." Even as Jack was writing of his own feelings at *his* mother's death, grief so clouded his memory that he was unable to recall them clearly—picturing his young self (and now Douglas and David) as heartless and unfeeling.

Jack had always believed emotion to be "something uncomfortable and embarrassing and even dangerous" (he had said so in the first paragraph of his autobiography). For sixty years, he had avoided it, believing that it would always, inevitably, bring him pain and suffering. Joy, however, had pried open the protective carapace and exposed the creature within; and it had proved a glorious and far from traumatic experience. Then, with unbelievable cruelty, pain and suffering *had* followed and, finding him for the first time defenseless and unprepared, were all the more devastating.

"I not only lived each endless day in grief," he wrote, "but I live each day thinking about living each day in grief . . . what am I to do?" The answer, for a writer, was to write. Day by day he began to record his feelings and emotions: "By writing it all down (all?—no: one thought in a hundred) I believe I get a little outside it. . . ."

Here, in the anonymous pages of a child's exercise book, the Christian apologist was free to express his doubts, the great teacher able to ask unanswerable questions:

> I look up at the night sky. Is anything more certain than that in all those vast times and spaces, if I were allowed to search them, I should nowhere find her face, her voice, her touch? She died. She is dead. Is the word so difficult to learn?

But it *was* difficult to learn, and except for his work—"where the machine seems to run on much as usual"—the difficulty of accepting Joy's death left him physically and mentally exhausted. Except for his jottings about grief, he was unable to write. He found it impossible to read, and simple daily tasks, such as shaving, seemed burdensome and unnecessary.

Then, suddenly, there would be times when it seemed to Jack that he might get over his grief, when the voice of common sense reminded him that he had been happy before he had met Joy, and insisted that he would, one day soon, be happy again. But the memory of what he had lost always returned: the commonsense arguments vanished "like an ant in the mouth of a furnace" and Jack was once more reduced to "a whimpering child":

> My heart and body are crying out, come back, come back. . . .
> But I know this is impossible. I know that the thing I want I
> can never get. The old life, the jokes, the drinks, the arguments,
> the love-making, the tiny, heartbreaking commonplace. . . .

It was this desperate yearning that he wrote of in a poem, cryptically entitled "Joys That Sting":

> To take the old walks alone, or not at all,
> To order one pint where I ordered two,
> To think of, and then not to make, the small
> Time-honoured joke (senseless to all but you);
>
> To laugh (oh, one'll laugh), to talk upon
> Themes that we talked upon when you were there,
> To make some poor pretence of going on,
> Be kind to one's old friends, and seem to care,
>
> While no one (O God) through the years will say
> The simplest, common word in just your way. . . .

People expected Jack to find consolation in his faith, but he couldn't:

> Talk to me about the truth of religion and I'll listen gladly.
> Talk to me about the duty of religion and I'll listen submis-

sively. But don't come talking to me about the consolations of religion or I shall suspect that you don't understand.

Time and again he constructed complex arguments of faith only to find them demolished by his grief as if they were no more than a house of cards.

A door had been slammed shut, locked, barred, and double-bolted (or so it seemed) from the inside. No amount of knocking brought a reply. Jack found that he did not even have a good photograph of Joy by which to remember her, and while the face of a stranger passed in the street would return suddenly and vividly to his mind, he could not properly recall the face of the woman he loved. His attempts to pray to God about Joy were like "speaking into a vacuum about a nonentity." It was a vacuum sucked out by Jack's anger and bitterness toward God:

What chokes every prayer and every hope is the memory of all the prayers we offered and all the false hopes we had. Not hopes raised merely by our own wishful thinking; hopes encouraged, even forced upon us, by false diagnoses, by x-ray photographs, by strange remissions, by one temporary recovery that might have ranked as a miracle. Step by step we were "led up the garden path." Time after time, when He seemed most gracious He was really preparing the next torture. . . .

Jack had arrived, more by anguish than by logic, at an extraordinary theory: supposing God were bad? Supposing men were nothing more than rats trapped in the laboratory of a mad celestial vivisectionist?

The idea was conceived in the passion of pain—it was, said Jack, "a yell rather than a thought"—but it had to be argued through nevertheless. "Is it rational," he asked, "to believe in a bad God? Anyway, in a God so bad as all that? The Cosmic Sadist, the spiteful imbecile?" No, he decided, it was not. To do so would be to wipe God off the slate, and there would then be

> no motive for obeying him. Not even fear. . . . If cruelty is from this point of view 'good'. . . what He calls 'Heaven' might well be what we should call Hell, and vice-versa. . . .

Many of Jack's admirers would have been deeply shocked if they had known that he had even entertained such doubts, or admitted such fears. In a sense, it shocked Jack himself—"Why do I make room in my mind for such filth and nonsense?"—but it was only by confronting his worst imaginings that he could overcome them.

Day by day, as he wrote about his grief, his conception of God began to change. There was nothing in the nature of God's dealing with him that was experimental:

> God has not been trying an experiment on my faith or love, in order to find out their quality. He knew it already. It was I who didn't. In this trial He makes us occupy the dock, the witness box, and the bench all at once. He always knew my temple was a house of cards. His only way of making me realize the fact was to knock it down. . . .

A note of peace began to enter the writings with which he had now filled three exercise books:

> I have gradually been coming to feel that the door is no longer shut and bolted. Was it my own frantic need that slammed it in my face? The time when there is nothing at all in your soul except a cry for help may be just the time when God can't give it: you are like a drowning man who can't be helped because he clutches and grabs. Perhaps your own reiterated cries deafen you to the voice you hoped to hear. . . .

Two months after Joy's death, he wrote to his American lady correspondent who had asked how he took his sorrow:

The answer is "In nearly all possible ways." Because, as you probably know, it isn't a state but a process. It keeps on changing—like a winding road with quite a new landscape at each bend.

He had made, however, two important discoveries in traveling this road: one was his realization that the times when he most loudly called to God for help were when he never received it; the other was that "the moments at which I feel nearest to Joy are precisely those when I mourn her *least*." It was as if "clamorous need seems to shut one off from the thing needed. It is almost like '*Don't* knock and it shall be opened to you'...."

In the fourth and last exercise book he wrote:

These notes have been about myself, and about Joy, and about God. In that order. The order and the proportions exactly what they ought not to have been.

Once he had come to this conclusion, he suddenly found the door no longer locked. If God didn't answer his unanswerable human questions about suffering and grief it was, at least,

a rather special sort of "No answer" ... more like a silent, certainly not uncompassionate, gaze. As though He shook His head not in refusal but waiving the question. Like, "Peace, child; you don't understand."

As Orual says at the end of *Till We Have Faces*:

I know now, Lord, why you utter no answer. You are yourself the answer. Before your face questions die away. What other answer would suffice? Only words, words, words; to be led out to battle against other words....

Jack's expressions of raw emotion gave place to a logically argued, and poetically described, analysis of the nature of bereavement. When a loved one dies, he wrote, "we think of this

177

as love cut short; like a dance stopped in mid career or flower with its head unluckily snapped off—something truncated and therefore, lacking its due shape," whereas it is really

> a universal and integral part of our experience of love. It follows marriage as normally as marriage follows courtship or as autumn follows summer. It is not a truncation of the process but one of its phases; not the interruption of the dance but the next figure.

Bereavement, Jack decided, was a potentially dangerous state in which the bereaved can so easily "fall back to loving our past, or our memory, or our sorrow, or our relief from sorrow, or our own love."

With the restoration of his faith, Jack looked for a new way to describe Joy. He eventually adopted a much-loved simile; Joy, he wrote, was

> like a garden. Like a nest of gardens, wall within wall, hedge within hedge, more secret, more full of fragrant and fertile life the further you entered. . . . In some way, in its unique way, like Him who made it.

Then, at last, he was able to turn his gaze "from the garden to the Gardener. . . . To the life-giving Life and the Beauty that makes beautiful."

Jack began to rediscover a greater truth still, a truth of which he had written—twenty years before—in the mystical conclusion to *Perelandra*:

> All that is made seems planless to the darkened mind, because there are more plans than it looked for. . . . So with the Great Dance. . . . plans without number interlock, and each movement becomes in its season the breaking into flower of the whole design. . . . Set your eyes on one movement and it will lead you through all patterns and it will seem to you the master movement. But the seeming will be true. There seems

no plan because it is all plan: there seems no centre because
it is all centre. . . .

Gradually, Jack achieved a clearer perspective. Difficulties
in communication began to ease, especially with Douglas,
whom he now described as being "the greatest comfort to
me." Slowly the old man and the young boy overcame their
individual inhibitions and began to talk together about Joy
and "to look back lovingly at the happy times."

There were so many joys to be remembered, often so seem-
ingly inconsequential that they had been buried beneath the
avalanche of grief: games of Scrabble played simultaneously
in English, French, Latin, and Greek; the cut and thrust of
argument; long walks followed by pints of ale in old pubs; talk
of books and bookmen—George MacDonald, Jane Austen,
Dr. Johnson, H. G. Wells, and Samuel Pepys; music—Mozart
and Chopin—played by Joy on the specially hired piano at
the Kilns; poetry, read aloud: *The Iliad* to stir the spirit, or
the wistful verses of A. E. Housman, over which they often
wept together, or that sonnet by Shakespeare, so particularly
apposite:

> Music to hear, why hear'st thou music sadly?
> Sweets with sweets war not, joy delights in joy:
> Why lov'st thou that which thou receiv'st not gladly,
> Or else receiv'st with pleasure thine annoy?
> If the true concord of well-tuned sounds,
> By unions married, do offend thine ear
> They do but sweetly chide thee, who confounds
> In singleness the parts that thou shouldst bear.
> Mark how one string, sweet husband to another,
> Strikes each in each by mutual ordering;
> Resembling sire, and child, and happy mother,
> Who, all in one, one pleasing note do sing:
> > Whose speechless song, being many, seeming one,
> > Sings this to thee thou single wilt prove none.

In September, Jack felt able to talk over some of his recent experiences with his friend Roger Lancelyn Green. He even told Roger that he had been writing about his feelings of grief, adding—under pledge of secrecy—that he might possibly publish what he had written, in the hope that it might help others in bereavement.

This he did, in 1961, under the title *A Grief Observed*; Joy's identity was disguised by the initial H. (Joy's first name was Helen.) Today, *A Grief Observed* is one of C. S. Lewis's best-selling books, but his name did not appear on the work until after his death; it was published under the pseudonym of N. W. Clerk. Jack had often used the initials N. W., or the name "Nat Whilk" on contributions to the *Oxford Magazine* and later *Punch*. The name was derived from the Anglo-Saxon *nat whilc*, meaning "I know not whom." "Clerk," taken again from Anglo-Saxon, simply implied a scholar, one able to read and write.

The reviewer of the *Times Literary Supplement* wrote:

> Begun after his wife's death from a long and painful illness, the Journal might itself have become an instrument of escape. But its honest dissection is the negation of self-pity. Honest it is; but too complex, intellectualized and indeed well-written to be artless in the sense of naive. Drawing firmly back from each conventional posture of the mourner, Mr. Clerk invites not sympathy but co-operation in his attempt to argue out a grief.

Mr. Lewis carried the process further: "He came to realise," says Douglas Gresham,

> that grief was a selfish thing: he wasn't crying because Joy had gone somewhere else, he was crying because he didn't have her anymore. It takes a great deal of thought and courage to face up to the fact that what you are grieving over is that you have lost someone, not that something has happened to them.

180

What had happened to Joy was that she had been set free: free from the endless battle against an insidious disease; free from the pain and the agony; and free from the torment of waiting for death. For Jack the pain went on.

"He overcame his grief," says Douglas, "to the extent that he could function again as a human being and as a writer—but there was never, ever, any time at which he wasn't conscious of his loss."

Jack had enjoyed a harmony with Joy:

> The most precious gift that marriage gave me was this constant impact of something very close and intimate yet all the time unmistakably other, resilient—in a word, real. . . . No cranny of heart or body remained unsatisfied.

They had been, as the Bible calls it, one flesh—or, as Jack described it, one ship.

The ship of their love had had a rough passage through cruel seas. The storms were over, but they had taken their toll: "The starboard engine has gone. I, the port engine, must chug along somehow till we make harbour. . . ."

11

Further Up and Further In

It was the Unicorn who summed up what everyone was feeling. He stamped his right fore-hoof on the ground and neighed and then cried: "I have come home at last! This is my real country! I belong here. This is the land I have been looking for all my life, though I never knew it till now. . . . Come further up, come further in!"

It was five years since Jack had written *The Last Battle* and sent the characters of Narnia across the frontier into Aslan's country. In those five years, he had fallen in love with, married, and lost the woman whom he described as: "my daughter, my mother, my pupil and my teacher, my subject and my sovereign . . . my trusty comrade, friend, shipmate, fellow-soldier. . . ."

Like Jewel the Unicorn, Joy had now found her way to the land where she belonged. Jack, however, had been left in the shadowlands.

He was sixty-three years old and had lived nine-tenths of his life without even knowing this woman who had turned his world upside down. Yet he could never now completely return to the life he had lived before. He wrote: "Did you even know, dear, how much you took away with you when you left? You have stripped me even of my past, even of the things we never shared...."

In his correspondence, Jack began to write often of death, adding the initals DV to any arrangements he made or plans he talked of. Writing to his oldest of friends, Arthur Greeves, with whom he had a marvelously happy reunion in 1961, Jack remarked that "the party gets thinner and I suppose you and I shall be leaving it soon." To his American lady friend, he described his body as being like an old automobile "where all sorts of apparently different things keep going wrong. What they add up to is the plain fact that the machine is wearing out. Well, it was not meant to last forever. Still," he added nostalgically, "I have a kindly feeling for the old rattletrap...."

The machine really was wearing out. In the summer of 1961, Jack was diagnosed as suffering from a diseased prostate gland, but problems with his kidneys and his heart made it impossible for the surgeons to operate. He was forced to wear a catheter, live on a low-protein diet, and sleep downstairs in a chair.

A few months later, in October, he was in and out of the hospital for blood transfusions, an experience which prompted the observation: "Dracula must have led a horrid life." He was better for a short time, but then had a relapse from which it took him a long time to recover. "Apparently," he told T. S. Eliot the following spring, "I shall always be an invalid—but I have no pain and feel tolerably well."

He remained, however, too ill for the operation, and problems with his heart and difficulties with his "plumbing" considerably restricted his activities:

No more bathing or real walks, and as few stairs as possible. A very mild fate: especially since nature seems to remove the desire for excercise when the power declines.

After writing *A Grief Observed*, Jack entered a twilight phase: outwardly, he showed much of the same old wit and intellectual bravado, tempered now by a new peace and a deeper sense of humanity; inwardly, he was restless, itching to be off on a journey of his own.

Years before, when writing *Surprised by Joy*, he had said: "All Joy reminds. It is never a possession, always a desire for something longer ago or further away, or still about to be." Again and again, he had tried to pin down this elusive emotion: "All your life," he had written in *The Problem of Pain*,

> an unattainable ecstasy has hovered just beyond the grasp of your consciousness. The day is coming when you will wake to find, beyond all hope, that you have attained it, or else, that it was within your reach and you have lost it forever.

It increasingly seemed to Jack that this ecstasy, this joy was really a glimpse of something otherworldly; something which—because it carried the label "death"—has been universally misunderstood, feared rather than desired.

In *Till We Have Faces*, Psyche confides to her sister:

> I have always—at least, ever since I can remember—had a kind of longing for death. . . . It was when I was happiest that I longed most. It was on those happy days when we were up on the hills, with the wind and the sunshine. . . . Do you remember? The colour and the smell, and looking across at the Grey Mountain in the distance? And because it was so beautiful, it set me longing, always longing. Everything seemed to be saying, Psyche come! But I couldn't come and I didn't know where I was to come to. It almost hurt me. I felt like a bird in a cage when the other birds of its kind are flying home. . . .

Jack still managed to get to Cambridge some weeks and to attend the Monday meetings of the Inklings survivors which now met at the Lamb and Flag (the "Bird and Baby" having become "intolerably cold, dark, noisy and child-pestered").

185

The following year, Jack was working on several projects: there was *The Discarded Image*, edited from a series of lectures on Medieval and Renaissance Literature which he had given in 1938. (Dedicated to Roger Lancelyn Green, the book was posthumously published in 1964.)

He had been working at the book, on and off, for several years. In 1957, Joy had told Bill that Jack was writing "a fearsome work of scholarship" which resulted in his going about "muttering bits of Latin and Anglo-Saxon, except when the cat trips him up, when what he says is much more vernacular!" Jack was also collecting together some of his miscellaneous sermons, essays, and addresses. The first volume, *They Asked for a Paper*, appeared in 1962; the second—which Jack had called *A Slip of the Tongue*—was published, after his death, as *Screwtape Proposes a Toast*. He had also begun to write *Letters to Malcolm*, a book about prayer.

These largely magpie activities were prompted partly no doubt by the conviction that his life was drawing to a close, but also because he had a very real fear that sales of his books would decline when he died. He was anxious to publish as much as he could in the hope that he would be able to leave sufficient income for the support of his brother and his stepsons.

Despite Jack's indifferent health, life at the Kilns was particularly pleasant for him at this time. Douglas was now studying at Magdalen School, Oxford, and so was living at home; Warnie was manfully fighting his alcoholism (proudly recording in his diary that during 1961 he had been a teetotaller for 355 days); and Jack still received visitors and guests, with whom he would often sit up talking until midnight.

There were still the cats: "We are ruled by cats," he wrote,

Joy's Siamese—my "stepcat" as I call her—is the most terribly conversational animal I ever knew. She talks all the time and wants doors and windows to be opened for her 1000 times an hour. . . . She adores me because I lift her up by her tail—an

operation which I can't imagine I should like if I were a cat,
but she comes back for more and more, purring all the time. . . .
How strange that God brings us into such intimate relations
with creatures of whose real purpose and destiny we remain
forever ignorant. . . .

In September 1962, Jack received news that must have given
him much pause for thought. Bill Gresham had died in New
York City. He had had cancer.

Two months later, Jack heard with anxiety that Arthur
Greeves was suffering from heart trouble. His reply was telling:
"I know what it's like," he wrote, "gasping like a new-caught
fish which no one has the kindness to knock on the head."

Arthur's illness was a bitter blow to Jack because, despite
his own state of health ("still catheterised and still on a low-
protein diet"), he had thought of arranging a trip to Ireland,
with Douglas, the following summer so as to spend some time
with his old friend again.

Arthur's condition, however, improved, and plans for the
visit began to be made in earnest, with Jack sending Arthur
names and addresses of possible hotels and adding: "Keep our
fingers crossed and keep saying D V."

Early in 1963, Jack received a visit from Walter Hooper, a
young American from the University of Kentucky, who had
come to England to research and write a critical study of him.
Though apprehensive at meeting the man whose work he
admired, Walter Hooper found Jack's welcome at the Kilns
"so bright, loud and jovial that I quickly forgot my fright. We
went into his sitting-room and were soon talking about—well,
what seemed like everything under the sun." The meeting
went famously, others followed, and the two men had soon
struck up a cordial friendship. Walter was introduced to the
Monday gatherings at the Lamb and Flag, and Jack gave what
help he could with the research, although he didn't entirely
approve of books being written about living authors in general
and himself in particular.

Jack was a modest man who had long ago come to the conclusion that "the essential vice, the utmost evil, is Pride." In *Mere Christianity*, he wrote that it was the

> one vice of which no man in the world is free; which everyone in the world loathes when he sees it in someone else; and of which hardly any people, except Christians, ever imagine that they are guilty themselves. . . .

By the end of his life, Jack had achieved a staggeringly wide public reputation and had been awarded numerous academic honors: he was an honorary fellow of University and Magdalen Colleges, Oxford, and of Magdalene College, Cambridge; honorary doctor of divinity of St. Andrews University; honorary doctor of literature of Manchester University; recipient of the doctorate of literature from Laval University, Quebec; fellow of the British Academy and of the Royal Society of Literature; winner of the Gollancz Memorial Prize for Literature and the Carnegie Medal for the best children's book of 1956 (*The Last Battle*).

He had, however, courteously declined the more public honor of Commander of the British Empire which was offered him in 1951. Jack's reputation meant a great deal more to others than it did to him, and he rarely reread or spoke about his own writings. Otherwise, he would talk to anyone about anything, and had the singular gift of not merely listening to other people, but of making them feel they had something of value to say.

Jack's long-standing friend Owen Barfield has written:

> Throughout the whole of his life I never recall a single remark, a single word or silence, a single look, the lightest flicker of an eyelid or hemi-demi-semitone of alteration in the pitch of his voice, which would go to suggest that he felt his opinion entitled to more respect than that of old friends he was talking with because unlike theirs, it had won the ear of tens of hundreds of thousands wherever the English language is

spoken and in a good many places where it is not. I wonder how many famous men there have been of whom this could truthfully be said.

It was for Jack simply a prerequisite of his faith that he should fight against what he saw as the "spiritual cancer" of pride. "A proud man," he once remarked, "is always looking down on things and people: and, of course, as long as you are looking down, you cannot see something that is above you. . . ."

And, all too conscious of the fact that "a man is never so proud as when striking an attitude of humility," he wrote the following poem entitled "The Apologist's Evening Prayer":

> From all my lame defeats and oh! Much more
> From all the victories that I seemed to score;
> From cleverness shot forth on Thy behalf
> At which, while angels weep, the audience laugh;
> From all my proofs of Thy divinity,
> Thou, who wouldst give no sign, deliver me
> Thoughts are but coins. Let me not trust, instead
> Of Thee, their thin-worn image of Thy head.
> From all my thoughts, even from my thoughts of Thee,
> O thou fair Silence, fall, and set me free.
> Lord of the narrow gate and the needle's eye,
> Take from me all my trumpery lest I die.

In March 1963, arrangements were finalized for Jack and Douglas's trip to Ireland. "Bravo!" he wrote to Arthur. "We're too old to let our remaining chances slip!"

Three months later he was writing to his American lady friend who was facing a serious operation with great fear:

> Remember, tho' we struggle against things because we are afraid of them, it is often the other way round—we get afraid *because* we struggle. Are you struggling, resisting? Don't you think Our Lord says to you "Peace, child, peace. Relax. Let go.

Underneath you are the everlasting arms. Let go, I will catch you. Do you trust me so little?"

"Of course," he concluded, "this may not be the end. Then make it a good rehearsal." The letter was signed "Yours (and like you a tired traveller, near the journey's end) Jack."

By the beginning of July he was writing to tell her that his own ill-health had returned and that he was waiting for the doctor's decision on whether or not he could go to Ireland. "Our friends," he added wryly, "might really get up a sweepstake as to whose train really will go first!"

Two days later, on July 11, he sent a short note to Arthur Greeves: "Alas! I have had a collapse as regards the heart trouble and the holiday has to be cancelled. . . . I don't mind—or not much—missing the jaunt, but it is a blow missing *you*."

In his inaugural lecture at Cambridge in 1954, he had told his audience:

> . . . Where I fail as a critic, I may yet be useful as a specimen. I would even dare to go further. Speaking not only for myself but for all other Old Western men whom you may meet, I would say, use your specimens while you can. There are not going to be many more dinosaurs.

Waiting for admission to the Acland, he wrote to a friend: "I am but a *fossil* dinosaur now."

On Sunday, July 14, Walter Hooper arrived at the Kilns to accompany Jack to church. He found him wearing his dressing gown and looking very ill, unable to hold a cup or cigarette. He asked Walter if he would become his private secretary and stay in England and offered to pay him what he received from his American university. Walter accepted.

The following morning, Jack was admitted to the hospital. At 5:00 p.m. that day he had a heart attack. On Tuesday, he was unconscious and dying. At two o'clock in the afternoon, the end seemed near. Since Jack was still in a coma and therefore unable to receive the sacrament of Holy Communion, the curate of St. Mary Magdalen's anointed him with oil according to the service of Extreme Unction. Suddenly and inexplicably, Jack woke up and asked for his tea.

Walter Hooper and Austin Farrer arrived at the hospital later to find Jack "looking as though he'd woken from a twenty-year sleep." He asked why everyone looked so anxious and, on being told that he had been asleep for a long time, replied, "I do not think that it could be argued that I am a very *well* man!"

For days he was very far from well. An infection in his kidneys poisoned his bloodstream, and he was often confused, sometimes delirious. Writing on Jack's behalf to the American lady correspondent, Walter described him as being "vividly aware of living in a world of hallucinations"; and Jack himself later told Arthur Greeves that he had "all sorts of delusions. Very quaint ones some of them, but none painful or terrifying."

Eventually, Jack recovered sufficiently to go home to the Kilns where a bedroom was made for him downstairs and where he was attended by a resident male nurse. It became clear that he would not be able to return to Cambridge. In a dictated letter (he found it difficult to hold a pen), he told Roger Lancelyn Green: "I am now unofficially an extinct volcano, i.e. I have resigned the Chair and Fellowship."

The next two months passed quietly and peacefully. The proofs of Jack's book on prayer, *Letters to Malcolm*, arrived and were checked for publication. For those who suppose from reading *A Grief Observed* that Jack had lost his faith, *Letters to Malcolm* stands as a vivid testimony to the contrary. Writing of his belief in life after death, he said:

> ... The hills and valleys of Heaven will be to those you now experience not as a copy is to an original, nor as a substitute to the genuine article, but as the flower to the root, or the diamond to the coal. ...

Then the new earth and sky, the same yet not the same as these, will rise in us as we have risen in Christ. And once again, after who knows what aeons of the silence and the dark, the birds will sing out and the waters flow, and lights and shadows move across the hills and the faces of our friends laugh upon us with amazed recognition.

Guesses, of course, only guesses. If they are not true, something better will be. For we know that we shall be made like Him, for we shall see Him as He is.

In September, Walter Hooper went back to America to settle his affairs before returning to take up his responsibilities as Jack's secretary. He was to never see him again.

In his absence Jack handled his own correspondence once more, writing what were to be the last letters to his two most prolific correspondents. To his first true friend and companion, Arthur Greeves, he wrote:

> Tho' I am by no means unhappy I can't help feeling it was rather a pity I did revive in July. I mean, having been glided so painlessly up to the Gate it seems hard to have it shut in one's face and know that the whole process must some day be gone thro' again, and perhaps less pleasantly! Poor Lazarus! But God knows best. I am glad you are fairly well. . . . But oh Arthur, never to see you again!

To the American lady, to whom he had written over 130 letters but had never met, he wrote: "I am quite comfortable but very easily tired. . . . So you must expect my letters to be very few and very short. More a wave of the hand than a letter. . . ."

The one sadness Jack found difficult to bear at this time was the absence of his brother. Warnie had gone to Ireland for his usual summer holiday and, on hearing of Jack's heart attack, began drinking heavily once more. Unwilling to face the fact that Jack was dying, he ignored pleas from friends to come home or at least write to his brother. He finally relented and returned in September. Instantly regretting his behavior, he did all in his power to comfort and care for Jack. Warnie wrote,

> Early in October it became apparent to both of us that he was facing death. In their way these last weeks were not unhappy. Joy had left us, and once again—as in the earliest days—we could turn for comfort only to each other. The wheel had come full circle.

In *Surprised by Joy*, Jack had recalled how he and Warnie had endured the worst excesses of their early school days by anticipating the holidays, and how, conversely, every holiday came to be haunted by the approaching menace of another term.

"Once again," wrote Warnie of their last days together, "we were shutting out from our talk the ever present knowledge that the holidays were ending, and a new term fraught with unknown possibilities awaited us both."

During November, a number of Jack's friends visited him, each leaving with the feeling that they had been to say *farewell*. Arthur Farrer wrote,

> The life Lewis had lived with zest he surrendered with composure. He was put almost beside himself by his wife's death; he seemed easy at the approach of his own.

The last guest to stay with Jack at the Kilns was Roger Lancelyn Green. Leaving, he said good-bye to Jack in the certain knowledge that it was "goodbye indeed."

A few days later, Jack made a final visit to the Lamb and Flag. Only one of his old friends, Colin Hardie, was there—but *he* was to remember that day as being "perhaps the best of all such Mondays."

Although Jack had told Warnie, "I have done all I wanted to do, and I'm ready to go," there was one small task left undone. The Chronicles of Narnia had grown and developed as they were written, and because Jack had possessed no clear overall plan when he began, there were several small discrepancies within the chronology which he was anxious to correct. So he had invited Kaye Webb, editor of Puffin Books, to call on him to discuss how he might reedit the stories.

When Kaye Webb called at the Kilns on November 21, Jack received her wearing his suit over his pajamas. They had a preliminary discussion about what changes needed to be made, and Kaye agreed to come back and see him again when he had completed the work.

Jack talked about the holiday with Joy in Greece and of the great happiness it had brought them.

> I stayed talking with him until seven when he said he felt tired. He told me he was almost disappointed that the heart-attack hadn't taken him. Then, the next day, I read that he had had another. . . .

"Friday, November 22," wrote Warnie, "began no differently from any other day for some weeks past."

> I looked in on Jack soon after six, got a cheerful "I'm all right" and then went about my domestic tasks. He got up at eight and, as usual, breakfasted in the kitchen in his dressing-gown, after which he took a preliminary survey of his cross-word puzzle. By the time he was dressed I had his mail ready for him, and he sat down in his work-room where he answered four letters with his own hand. For some time past he had been finding great difficulty in keeping awake, and finding him asleep in his chair after lunch, I suggested that he would be more comfortable in bed. He agreed, and went there. At four o'clock I took him in his tea and had a few words with him, finding him thick in his speech, very drowsy, but calm and cheerful. It was the last time we ever spoke to each other.

194

A few months before, Jack had written of old age:

Think of yourself just as a seed patiently waiting in the earth;
waiting to come up a flower in the Gardener's good time,
up into the *real* world, the real waking. I suppose that our
whole present life, looked back on from there, will seem only
a drowsy half-waking. We are here in the land of dreams. But
cock-crow is coming. . . .

At five-thirty, Warnie heard a crash in Jack's bedroom
and, running in, "found him lying unconscious at the foot
of the bed. He ceased to breathe some three or four minutes
later. The following Friday would have been his sixty-fifth
birthday. . . ."

Recalling the unique qualities that had made up the character of C. S. Lewis, Austin Farrer wrote:

He took in more, he felt more, he remembered more, he in-
vented more. . . . His writings record an intense awareness,
a vigorous reaction, a taking of the world into his heart. . . .
His blacks and whites of good and evil and his ecstasies and
miseries were the tokens of a capacity for experience beyond
our scope. . . .

Jack's funeral was held at Headington Quarry Parish Church
on November 26, 1963, a cold, frosty, sunny day. Warnie was
too distraught to attend. Peter Bayley retained a vivid memory
of the occasion:

There was one candle on the coffin as it was carried out into
the churchyard. It seemed not only appropriate but also a
symbol of the man and his integrity and his absoluteness and
his faith that the flame burned so steadily, even in the open
air, and seemed so bright, even in the bright sun.

Later, a simple stone was laid, bearing a cross and an inscription chosen by Warnie:

IN LOVING MEMORY OF
MY BROTHER
CLIVE STAPLES LEWIS
BORN BELFAST 29TH NOVEMBER 1898
DIED IN THIS PARISH
22ND NOVEMBER 1963
MEN MUST ENDURE THEIR GOING HENCE

These words, taken from the fifth act of *King Lear*, had a particular signficance for Jack and Warnie. When their mother died on August 23, 1908, Warnie recalled,

> There was a Shakespearean calendar hanging on the wall of the room where she died, and my father preserved for the rest of his life the leaf for that day, with its quotation: "Men must endure their going hence."

During his final illness, Jack had composed and dictated an epitaph for Joy that was inscribed on a cruciform plaque and placed in the crematorium:

Remember
HELEN JOY
DAVIDMAN
D. JULY 1960
Loved wife of
C. S. Lewis

Here the whole world (stars, water, air,
And field, and forest, as they were
Reflected in a single mind)
Like cast off clothes was left behind
In ashes, yet with hope that she,
Re-born from holy poverty,
In lenten lands, here after may
Resume them on her Easter Day.

Then Aslan turned to them and said:

"You do not yet look so happy as I mean you to be."

Lucy said, "We're so afraid of being sent away, Aslan. And you have sent us back into our own world so often."

"No fear of that," said Aslan. "Have you not guessed? . . . all of you are—as you used to call it in the Shadowlands—dead. The term is over; the holidays have begun. The dream is ended: this is the morning."

And as He spoke He no longer looked to them like a lion; but the things that began to happen after that were so great and beautiful that I cannot write them. And for us this is the end of all the stories, and we can most truly say that they all lived happily ever after. But for them it was only the beginning of the real story. All their life in this world and all their adventures in Narnia had only been the cover and the title-page: now at last they were beginning Chapter One of the Great Story which no one on earth has read: which goes on forever: in which every chapter is better than the one before.

C. S. Lewis
The Last Battle

Bibliography of Works by C. S. Lewis, Joy Davidman, William Lindsay Gresham, and W. H. Lewis

Where possible, books have been listed by the American publishers.

C. S. Lewis

The Abolition of Man. New York: Macmillan, 1962.

Allegory of Love: A Study of Medieval Tradition. New York: Oxford Univ. Press, 1936.

With Charles Williams, *Arthurian Torso.* London: Oxford Univ. Press, 1948.

Boxen: The Imaginary World of the Young C. S. Lewis. Edited by Walter Hooper. Orlando, Fla.: Harcourt, Brace, Jovanovich, 1985.

Christian Reflections. Grand Rapids, Mich.: Wm. B. Eerdmans, 1974.

The Dark Tower and Other Stories. Edited by Walter Hooper. New York: Harcourt, Brace, Jovanovich, 1977.

The Discarded Image. New York: Cambridge Univ. Press, 1968.

Dymer. London: J. M. Dent, 1950.

English Literature in the Sixteenth Century. New York: Oxford Univ. Press, 1954.

Essays Presented to Charles Williams. Grand Rapids, Mich.: Wm. B. Eerdmans, 1966.

Experiment in Criticism. New York: Cambridge Univ. Press, 1961.

Fern-seed and Elephants, and Other Essays on Christianity. Edited by Walter Hooper. London: Fontana Books, 1976.

The Four Loves. New York: Harcourt, Brace, Jovanovich, 1971.

God in the Dock. Edited by Walter Hooper. Grand Rapids, Mich.: Wm. B. Eerdmans, 1970.

The Great Divorce. New York: Macmillan, 1978.

A Grief Observed. Macon, Ga.: Winston Press, 1963.

A Horse and His Boy. New York: Macmillan, 1969.

The Last Battle. New York: Macmillan, 1969.

Letters of C. S. Lewis. Edited by W. H. Lewis. London: Geoffrey Bles, 1966.

Letters to an American Lady. Edited by Clyde S. Kilby. Grand Rapids, Mich.: Wm. B. Eerdmans, 1967.

Letters to Malcolm: Chiefly on Prayer. New York: Harcourt, Brace, Jovanovich, 1973.

The Lion, the Witch and the Wardrobe. New York: Macmillan, 1968.

The Magician's Nephew. New York: Macmillan, 1970.

Mere Christianity. New York: Macmillan, 1964.

Miracles. New York: Macmillan, 1968.

Narrative Poems. Edited by Walter Hooper. New York: Harcourt, Brace, Jovanovich, 1979.

Of Other Worlds: Essays and Stories. Edited by Walter Hooper. New York: Harcourt, Brace, Jovanovich, 1975.

Out of the Silent Planet. New York: Macmillan, 1943.

Perelandra. New York: Macmillan, 1968.

With E. M. W. Tillyard. *The Personal Heresy: A Controversy.* London: Oxford Univ. Press, 1939.

The Pilgrim's Regress. Grand Rapids, Mich.: Wm. B. Eerdmans, 1958.

Poems. Edited by Walter Hooper. New York: Harcourt, Brace, Jovanovich, 1977.

Preface to Paradise Lost. New York: Oxford Univ. Press, 1942.

Prince Caspian. New York: Macmillan, 1969.

The Problem of Pain. New York: Macmillan, 1978.

Reflections on the Psalms. New York: Harcourt, Brace, Jovanovich, 1964.

Rehabilitations and Other Essays. Salem, N.H.: Ayer Co. Pubs., 1939.

The Screwtape Letters, With Screwtape Proposes a Toast. New York: Macmillan, 1964, 1967.

Selected Literary Essays. Edited by Walter Hooper. New York: Cambridge Univ. Press, 1969.

The Silver Chair. New York: Macmillan, 1967.

Spenser's Images of Life. Edited by A. Fowler. New York: Cambridge Univ. Press, 1967.

Spirits in Bondage: A Cycle of Lyrics. New York: Harcourt, Brace, Jovanovich, 1984.

Studies in Medieval and Renaissance Literature. New York: Cambridge Univ. Press, 1980.

Studies in Words. Rev. ed. New York: Cambridge Univ. Press, 1960.

Surprised by Joy: The Shape of My Early Life. New York: Harcourt, Brace, Jovanovich, 1956.

That Hideous Strength. New York: Macmillan, 1968.

They Asked for a Paper: Papers and Addresses. London: Geoffrey Bles, 1962.

They Stand Together: The Letters of C. S. Lewis to Arthur Greeves. Edited by Walter Hooper. London: Collins, 1979.

Till We Have Faces: A Myth Retold. New York: Harcourt, Brace, Jovanovich, 1980.

Transposition and Other Essays. London: Geoffrey Bles, 1949.

Undeceptions: Essays on Theology and Ethics. Edited by Walter Hooper. London: Geoffrey Bles, 1971.

The Voyage of the "Dawn Treader." New York: Macmillan, 1969.

The World's Last Night and Other Essays. New York: Harcourt, Brace, Jovanovich, 1973.

Edited by C. S. Lewis

George MacDonald: An Anthology. New York: Macmillan, 1978.

Joy Davidman

Anya. New York: Macmillan, 1940.

Letter to a Comrade. New Haven, Conn.: Yale Univ. Press, 1938.

"The Longest Way Round" in *These Found the Way: Thirteen Converts to Protestant Christianity.* Edited by David Wesley Soper. Philadelphia: Westminster Press, 1951.

(Contributed to) *Seven Poets in Search of an Answer.* Edited by Thomas Yoseloff. New York: Ackerman, 1944.

Smoke on the Mountain: An Interpretation of the Ten Commandments. Philadelphia: Westminster Press, 1953.

Weeping Bay. New York: Macmillan, 1950.

Edited by Joy Davidman

They Looked Like Men: The Poems of Alexander Bergman. New York: Ackerman, 1943.

War Poems of the United Nations. New York: Dial Press, 1943.

William Lindsay Gresham

The Book of Strength. London: Kaye and Ward, 1962.

"From Communist to Christian" in *These Found the Way: Thirteen Converts to Protestant Christianity.* Edited by David Wesley Soper. Philadelphia: Westminster Press, 1951.

Houdini: The Man Who Walked Through Walls. London: Gollancz, 1960.

Limbo Tower. New York: Rinehart, 1949.

Monster Midway: An Uninhibited Look at the Glittering World of the Carny. New York: Rinehart, 1953.

Nightmare Abbey. New York: Rinehart, 1946.

(Contributed to) *War Poems of the United Nations.* Edited by Joy Davidman. New York: Dial Press, 1943.

W. H. Lewis

Assault on Olympus: The Rise of the House of Gramont Between 1604 and 1678. London: Andre Deutsch, 1958.

Brothers and Friends: The Diaries of Major Warren Hamilton Lewis. Edited by Clyde S. Kilby and Marjorie Lamp Mead. San Francisco: Harper and Row, 1982.

"The Galleys of France" in *Essays Presented to Charles Williams*. Edited by C. S. Lewis. London: Oxford Univ. Press, 1947.

Levantine Adventurer: The Travels and Missions of the Chevalier d'Arvieux, 1653–1697. London: Andre Deutsch, 1962.

Louis XIV: An Informal Portrait. London: Andre Deutsch, 1959.

The Scandalous Regent: A Life of Philippe, Duc d'Orleans, 1674–1723, and of His Family. London: Andre Deutsch, 1961.

The Splendid Century: Some Aspects of French Life in the Reign of Louis XIV. London: Eyre and Spottiswoode, 1953.

The Sunset of the Splendid Century: The Life and Times of Louis Auguste de Bourbon, Duc de Maine, 1670–1736. London: Eyre and Spottiswoode, 1955.

Edited by W. H . Lewis

Letters of C. S. Lewis. London: Geoffrey Bles, 1966.

Memoirs of the Duc de Saint Simon. London: B. T. Batsford, 1964.

A Select List of Books about C. S. Lewis and Joy Davidman

Carpenter, Humphrey. *The Inklings: C. S. Lewis, J. R. R. Tolkien, Charles Williams and Their Friends*. New York: Ballantine, 1981.

Christensen, Michael. *C. S. Lewis on Scripture*. London: Hodder and Stoughton, 1979. (Foreword by Owen Barfield, Introduction by Clyde S. Kilby.)

Como, James T., ed. *C. S. Lewis at the Breakfast Table and Other Reminiscences*. New York: Macmillan, 1985. (Contributors include Peter Bayley, Austin Farrer, Roger Lancelyn Green, George Sayer, John Wain.)

Dorsett, Lyle W. *And God Came In: The Extraordinary Story of Joy Davidman*. New York: Macmillan, 1983.

Gibb, Jocelyn, ed. *Light on C. S. Lewis*. New York: Harcourt, Brace and World, 1965. (Contributors: Owen Barfield, Austin Farrer, J. A. W. Bennett, Nevill Coghill, John Lawlor, Stella Gibbons, Kathleen Raine, Chad Walsh, Walter Hooper.)

Gibson, Evan K. *C. S. Lewis: Spinner of Tales*. Ann Arbor, Mich.: Books on Demand, 1980.

Gilbert, Douglas, and Clyde S. Kilby. *C. S. Lewis: Images of His World*. Ann Arbor, Mich.: Books on Demand, 1979.

Green, Roger Lancelyn. *C. S. Lewis*. London: A Bodley Head Monograph, Bodley Head, 1963.

Green, Roger Lancelyn, and Walter Hooper. *C. S. Lewis: A Biography*. New York: Harcourt, Brace, Jovanovich, 1976.

Holmer, Paul L. *C. S. Lewis: The Shape of His Faith and Thoughts*. London: Sheldon Press, 1976.

Hooper, Walter. *Past Watchful Dragons: A Guide to C. S. Lewis's Chronicles of Narnia*. London: Fount-Collins, 1980.

Kilby, Clyde S. *Images of Salvation in the Fiction of C. S. Lewis*. Wheaton, Ill.: Harold Shaw Publishers, 1978.

Schakel, Peter J. *Reading With the Heart: The Way Into Narnia*. Grand Rapids, Mich.: Wm. B. Eerdmans, 1979.

Walsh, Chad. *C. S. Lewis: Apostle to the Skeptics*. New York: Macmillan, 1949.

Walsh, Chad. *The Literary Legacy of C. S. Lewis*. New York: Harcourt, Brace, Jovanovich, 1979.

Brian Sibley has written extensively about C. S. Lewis and Narnia as well as about Lewis's friend and fellow fantasy writer, J. R. R. Tolkien, and his imaginary kingdom, Middle-earth. Sibley dramatized the BBC's acclaimed radio versions of the Lord of the Rings and the Chronicles of Narnia and undertook extensive research for the TV movie *C. S. Lewis through the Shadowlands*. He lives in London.